INQUIRIES AND OPINIONS

BY

BRANDER MATTHEWS

Essay Index Reprint Series

BOOKS FOR LIBRARIES PRESS

FREEPORT, NEW YORK

First published 1907
Reprinted 1968

LIBRARY OF CONGRESS CATALOG CARD NUMBER:

68-22930

PRINTED IN THE UNITED STATES OF AMERICA

TO MY FRIEND AND FELLOW CRAFTSMAN
HENRY ARTHUR JONES

CONTENTS

LITERATURE IN THE NEW CENTURY

[This paper was read on September 24th, 1904, in the section of Belles-lettres of the International Congress of the Arts and Sciences, held at St. Louis.]

LITERATURE IN THE NEW CENTURY

THERE is no disguising the difficulty of any attempt to survey the whole field of literature as it is disclosed before us now at the opening of a new century; and there is no denying the danger of any effort to declare the outlook in the actual present and the prospect in the immediate future. How is it possible to project our vision, to foresee whither the current is bearing us, to anticipate the rocks ahead and the shallows whereon our bark may be beached?

But one reflection is as obvious as it is helpful. The problems of literature are not often merely literary; and, in so far as literature is an honest attempt to express life,—as it always has been at the moments of highest achievement,—the problems of literature must have an intimate relation to the problems which confront us insistently in life. If we turn from the disputations of the schools and look out on the world, we may discover forces at work in society which are exerting also a potent influence upon the future of literature.

3

Now that the century in which we were born and bred is receding swiftly into the past, we can perceive in the perspective more clearly than ever before its larger movements and its main endeavor. We are at last beginning to be able to estimate the heritage it has left us, and to see for ourselves what our portion is, what our possessions are, and what our obligations. While it is for us to make the twentieth century, no doubt, we need to remember that it was the nineteenth century which made us; and we do not know ourselves if we fail to understand the years in which we were molded to the work that lies before us. It is for us to single out the salient characteristics of the nineteenth century. It is for us to seize the significance of the striking advance in scientific method, for example, and of the wide-spread acceptance of the scientific attitude. It is for us, again, to recognize the meaning of that extension of the democratic movement, which is the most obvious characteristic of the past sixscore years. It is for us, once more, to weigh the importance of the intensifying of national spirit and of the sharpening of racial pride. And, finally, it is for us to take account also of the growth of what must be called " cosmopolitanism," that breaking down of the hostile barriers keeping one people apart from the others, ignorant of them, and often contemptuous.

4

Here, then, are four legacies from the nineteenth century to the twentieth:—first, the scientific spirit; second, the spread of democracy; third, the assertion of nationality; and, fourth, that stepping across the confines of language and race, for which we have no more accurate name than "cosmopolitanism."

I

"THE scientific spirit," so an acute American critic defined it recently in an essay on Carlyle,—who was devoid of it and detested it,—"the scientific spirit signifies poise between hypothesis and verification, between statement and proof, between appearance and reality. It is inspired by the impulse of investigation, tempered with distrust and edged with curiosity. It is at once avid of certainty and skeptical of seeming. It is enthusiastically patient, nobly literal, candid, tolerant, hospitable." This is the statement of a man of letters, who had found in science "a tonic force" stimulating to all the arts.

By the side of this, it may be well to set also the statement of a man of science. In his address delivered in St. Louis in December, 1903, the President of the American Association for the Advancement of Science,—who is also the president of one of the foremost of American univer-

5

sities, —declared that "the fundamental characteristic of the scientific method is honesty. . . . The sole object is to learn the truth and to be guided by the truth. Absolute accuracy, absolute fidelity, absolute honesty are the prime conditions of scientific progress." And then Dr. Remsen went on to make the significant assertion that "the constant use of the scientific method must in the end leave its impress upon him who uses it. A life spent in accord with scientific teaching would be of a high order. It would practically conform to the teachings of the highest type of religion."

This "use of the scientific method" is as remote as may be from that barren adoption of scientific phrases and that sterile application of scientific formulas, which may be dismissed as an aspect of "science falsely so called." It is of deeper import also than any mere utilization by art of the discoveries of science, however helpful this may be. The painter has been aided by science to perceive more precisely the effect of the vibrations of light and to analize more sharply the successive stages of animal movement; and the poet also has found his profit in the wider knowledge brought to us by later investigations. Longfellow, for example, drew upon astronomy for the figure with which he once made plain his moral:

Were a star quenched on high,
    For ages would its light,
Still travelling downward from the sky,
    Shine on our mortal sight.

So, when a great man dies,
    For years beyond our ken
The light he leaves behind him lies
    Upon the paths of men.

Wordsworth, a hundred years ago, warmly welcomed "the remotest discoveries of the chemist, the botanist and mineralogist," as "proper objects of the poet's art," declaring that "if the time should ever come when what is now called 'science,' thus familiarized to men, shall be ready to put on, as it were, a form of flesh and blood, the poet will lend his divine spirit to aid the transfiguration, and will welcome the being thus produced as a dear and genuine inmate of the household of man."

Again, the "use of the scientific method" is not equivalent to the application in the arts of scientific theories, altho here once more the man of letters is free to take these for his own and to bend them to his purpose. Ibsen has found in the doctrine of heredity a modern analog of the ancient Greek idea of fate; and altho he may not "see life steadily and see it whole," he has been enabled to invest his somber 'Ghosts' with not a little of the inexorable inevitability which we

7

feel to be so appalling in the master work of Sophocles. Criticism, no less than creation, has been stimulated by scientific hypothesis; and for one thing, the conception of literary history has been wholly transformed since the theory of evolution was declared. To M. Brunetière we owe the application of this doctrine to the development of the drama in his own language. He has shown us most convincingly how the several literary forms,—the lyric, the oration, the epic, with its illegitimate descendant, the modern novel in prose,—may cross-fertilize each other from time to time, and also how the casual hybrids that result are ever struggling to revert each to its own species.

Science is thus seen to be stimulating to art; but the "use of the scientific method" would seem to be more than stimulation only. It leads the practitioners of the several arts to set up an ideal of disinterestedness, inspired by a lofty curiosity, which shall scorn nothing as insignificant, and which is ever eager after knowledge ascertained for its own sake. As it abhors the abnormal and the freakish, the superficial and the extravagant, it helps the creative artist to strive for a more classic directness and simplicity; and it guides the critic toward passionless proportion and moderation. Altho it tends toward intellectual freedom, it forces us always to recognize the

8

reign of law. It establishes the strength of the social bond, and thereby, for example, it aids us to see that, altho romance is ever young and ever true, what is known as "neo-romanticism," with its reckless assertion of individual whim, is anti-social, and therefore probably immoral.

The "use of the scientific method" will surely strengthen the conscience of the novelist and of the dramatist; and it will train them to a sterner veracity in dealing with human character. It will inhibit that pitiful tendency toward a falsi-fication of the facts of life, which asserts the reform of a character in the twinkling of an eye just before the final fall of the curtain. It will lead to a renunciation of the feeble and summary psychology which permits a man of indurated habits of weakness or of wickedness to transform himself by a single and sudden effort of will. And, on the other hand, it may tempt certain stu-dents of life, subtler than their fellow-craftsmen and more inquisitive, to dwell unduly on the mere machinery of human motive and to aim not at a rich portrayal of the actions of men and women, but at an arid analysis of the mechanism of their impulses. More than one novelist of the twen-tieth century has already yielded to this tendency. No doubt, this is only the negative defect accom-panying a positive quality,—yet it indicates an imperfect appreciation of the artist's duty. "In

9

every art," so Taine reminded us, "it is necessary to linger long over the true in order to attain
the beautiful. The eye, fixing itself on an object,
begins by noting details with an excess of pre-
cision and fulness; it is only later, when the
inventory is complete, that the mind, master of
its wealth, rises higher, in order to take or to neglect what suits it."

The attitude of the literary critic will be modified by the constant use of the scientific method,
quite as much as the attitude of the literary
creator. He will seek to relate a work of art,
whether it is an epic or a tragedy, a novel or a
play, to its environment, weighing all the circumstances of its creation. He will strive to estimate it as it is, of course, but also as a contribution to the evolution of its species made by a
given people at a given period. He will endeavor
to keep himself free from lip-service and from
ancestor-worship, holding himself derelict to his
duty if he should fail to admit frankly that in
every masterpiece of the past, however transcend-
ent its merits, there must needs be much that is
temporary admixt with more that is permanent,—many things which pleased its author's
countrymen in his own time and which do not
appeal to us, even tho we can perceive also what
is eternal and universal, even tho we read into
every masterpiece much that the author's con-

temporaries had not our eyes to perceive. All
the works of Shakspere and of Molière are not of
equal value,—and even the finest of them is not
impeccable; and a literary critic who has a scientific sincerity will not gloss over the minor defects, whatever his desire to concentrate attention
on the nobler qualities by which Shakspere and
Molière achieved their mighty fame. Indeed, the
scientific spirit will make it plain that an unwav-
ering admiration for all the works of a great
writer, unequal as these must be of necessity, is
proof in itself of an obvious inability to perceive
wherein lies his real greatness.

Whatever the service the scientific spirit is
likely to render in the future, we need to be on
our guard against the obsession of science itself.
There is danger that an exclusive devotion to
science may starve out all interest in the arts, to
the impoverishment of the soul. Already there
are examples of men who hold science to be all-
sufficient and who insist that it has superseded
art. Already is it necessary to recall Lowell's
setting off of "art, whose concern is with the
ideal and the potential, from science which is
limited by the actual and the positive." Science
bids us go so far and no farther, despite the fact
that man longs to peer beyond the confines.
Vistas closed to science are opened for us by art;
and science fails us if we ask too much; for it

can provide no satisfactory explanation of the enigmas of existence. Above all, it tempts us to a hard and fast acceptance of its own formulas, an acceptance as deadening to progress as it is false to the scientific spirit itself. "History warns us," so Huxley declared, "that it is the customary fate of new truths to begin as heresies, and to end as superstitions."

II

THE growth of the scientific spirit is not more evident in the nineteenth century than the spread of the democratic movement. Democracy in its inner essence means not only the slow broadening down of government until it rests upon the assured foundation of the people as a whole, it signifies also the final disappearance of the feudal organization, of the system of caste, of the privileges which are not founded on justice, of the belief in any superiority conferred by the accident of birth. It starts with the assertion of the equality of all men before the law; and it ends with the right of every man to do his own thinking. Accepting the dignity of human nature, the democratic spirit, in its finer manifestations, is free from intolerance and rich in sympathy, rejoicing to learn how the other half lives. It is increasingly interested in human personality, in spite of the fact that humanity no longer bulks as big in the universe as it did before scientific discovery shattered the ancient assumption that the world had been made for man alone.

Perhaps, indeed, it is the perception of our own insignificance which is making us cling together more closely and seek to understand each other at least, even if we must ever fail to grasp the full import of the cosmic scheme. Whatever the reason, there is no gainsaying the growth of fellow-feeling and of a curiosity founded on friendly interest,—both of which are revealed far more abundantly in our later literatures than in the earlier classics. In the austere masterpieces of the Greek drama, for example, we may discover a lack of this warmth of sympathy; and we can not but suspect a certain aloofness, which is akin to callousness. The cultivated citizens of Athens were supported by slave-labor; but their great dramatic poets cast little light on the life of the slaves or on the sad conditions of their servitude. Something of this narrow chilliness is to be detected also in the literature of the court of Louis XIV; Corneille and Racine prefer to ignore not only the peasant but also the burgher; and it is partly because Molière's outlook on life is broader that the master of comedy appears to us now so much greater than his tragic contemporaries. Even of late the Latin races have seemed perhaps a little less susceptible to this appeal than the Teutonic or the Slavonic, and the impassive contempt of Flaubert and of Maupassant toward the creatures of their imaginative observation is more characteristic of the French attitude than the genial compassion of Daudet. In Hawthorne and in George Eliot there is no aristocratic remoteness; and Turgenieff and Tolstoi are innocent of haughty condescension. Everywhere now in the new century can we perceive the working of the democratic spirit, making literature more clearsighted, more tolerant, more pitying.

In his uplifting discussion of democracy, Lowell sought to encourage the timid souls who dreaded the danger that it might "reduce all mankind to a dead level of mediocrity" and that it might "lessen the respect due to eminence whether in station, virtue, or genius;" and he explained that, in fact, democracy meant a career open to talent, an opportunity equal to all, and therefore in reality a larger likelihood that genius would be set free. Here in America we have discovered by more than a century of experience that democracy levels up and not down; and that it is not jealous of a commanding personality even in public life, revealing a swift shrewdness of its own in gaging character, and showing both respect and regard for the independent leaders strong enough to withstand what may seem at the moment to be the popular will.

Nor is democracy hostile to original genius, or slow to recognize it. The people as a whole may throw careless and liberal rewards to the jesters and to the sycophants who are seeking its favor, as their forerunners sought to gain the ear of the monarch of old, but the authors of substantial popularity are never those who abase themselves or who scheme to cajole. At the beginning of the twentieth century there were only two writers whose new books appeared simultaneously in half a dozen different tongues; and what man has ever been so foolish as to call Ibsen and Tolstoi flatterers of humanity? The sturdy independence of these masters, their sincerity, their obstinate reiteration each of his own message,—these are main reasons for the esteem in which they are held. And in our own language, the two writers of widest renown are Mark Twain and Rudyard Kipling, known wherever English is spoken, in every remote corner of the seven seas, one an American of the Americans and the other the spokesman of the British Empire. They are not only conscientious craftsmen, each in his own way, but moralists also and even preachers; and they go forward in the path they have marked out, each for himself, with no swervings aside to curry favor or to avoid unpopularity.

The fear has been exprest freely that the position of literature is made more precarious by the recent immense increase in the reading public, deficient in standards of taste and anxious to be amused. It is in the hope of hitting the fancy of this motley body that there is now a tumultuous multiplication of books of every degree of merit; and amid all this din there must be redoubled difficulty of choice. Yet the selection gets itself made somehow, and not unsatisfactorily. Unworthy books may have vogue for a while, and even adulation; but their fame is fleeting. The books which the last generation transmitted to us were, after all, the books best worth our consideration; and we may be confident that the books we shall pass along to the next generation will be as wisely selected. Out of the wasteful overproduction only those works emerge which have in them something that the world will not willingly let die.

Those books that survive are always chosen from out the books that have been popular, and never from those that failed to catch the ear of their contemporaries. The poet who scorns the men of his own time and who retires into an ivory tower to inlay rimes for the sole enjoyment of his fellow mandarins, the poet who writes for posterity, will wait in vain for his audience. Never has posterity reversed the unfavorable verdict of an artist's own century. As Cicero said—and Cicero was both an aristocrat and an artist in letters,—"given time and opportunity, the recognition of the many is as necessary a test of excellence in an artist as that of the few." Verse, however exquisite, is almost valueless if its appeal is merely technical or merely academic, if it pleases only the sophisticated palate of the dilettant, if it fails to touch the heart of the plain people. That which vauntingly styles itself the *écriture artiste* must reap its reward promptly in praise from the *précieuses ridicules* of the hour. It may please those who pretend to culture without possessing even education; but this aristocratic affectation has no roots and it is doomed to wither swiftly, as one fad is ever fading away before another, as Asianism, euphuism, and Gongorism have withered in the past.

Fictitious reputations may be inflated for a little space; but all the while the public is slowly making up its mind; and the judgment of the main body is as trustworthy as it is enduring. 'Robinson Crusoe' and 'Pilgrim's Progress' hold their own generation after generation, altho the cultivated class did not discover their merits until long after the plain people had taken them to heart. Cervantes and Shakspere were widely popular from the start; and appreciative criticism limped lamely after the approval of the mob. Whatever blunders in belauding, the plain people may make now and again, in time they come unfailingly to a hearty appreciation of work that is honest, gen-

uine, and broad in its appeal; and when once
they have laid hold of the real thing they hold
fast with abiding loyalty.

III

As significant as the spread of democracy in
the nineteenth century is the success with which
the abstract idea of nationality has exprest itself
in concrete form. Within less than twoscore
years Italy has ceased to be only a geographical
expression; and Germany has given itself boundaries more sharply defined than those claimed
for the fatherland by the martial lyric of a century
ago. Hungary has asserted itself against the Aus-
trians, and Norway against the Swedes; and each
by the stiffening of racial pride has insisted on the
recognition of its national integrity. This is but
the accomplishment of an ideal toward which the
western world has been tending since it emerged
from the Dark Ages into the Renascence and since
it began to suspect that the Holy Roman Empire
was only the empty shadow of a disestablished
realm. In the long centuries the heptarchy in
England had been followed by a monarchy with
London for its capital; and in like manner the
seven kingdoms of Spain had been united under
monarchs who dwelt in Madrid. Normandy and
Gascony, Burgundy and Provence had been in-

corporated finally with the France of which the chief city was Paris.

Latin had been the tongue of every man who was entitled to claim benefit of clergy; but slowly the modern languages compacted themselves out of the warring dialects when race after race came to a consciousness of its unity and when the speech of a capital was set up at last as the standard to which all were expected to conform. In Latin Dante discust the vulgar tongue, tho he wrote the 'Divine Comedy' in his provincial Tuscan; yet Petrarch, who came after, was afraid that his poems in Italian were, by that fact, fated to be transitory. Chaucer made choice of the dialect of London, performing for it the service Dante had rendered to the speech of the Florentines; yet Bacon and Newton went back to Latin as the language still common to men of science. Milton practised his pen in Latin verse, but never hesitated to compose his epic in English. Latin served Descartes and Spinoza, men of science again; and it was not until the nineteenth century that the invading vernaculars finally ousted the language of the learned which had once been in universal use. And even now Latin is retained by the church which still styles itself Catholic.

It was as fortunate as it was necessary that the single language of the learned should give way before the vulgar tongues, the speech of the people, each in its own region best fitted to phrase the feelings and the aspirations of races dissimilar in their characteristics and in their ideals. No one tongue could voice the opposite desires of the northern peoples and of the southern; and we see the several modern languages revealing by their structure as well as by their vocabularies the essential qualities of the races that fashioned them, each for its own use. Indeed, these racial characteristics are so distinct and so evident to us now that we fancy we can detect them even tho they are disguised in the language of Rome; and we find significance in the fact that Seneca, the grandiloquent rhetorician, was by birth a Spaniard, and that Petronius, the robust realist, was probably born in what is now France.

The segregation of nationality has been accompanied by an increasing interest in the several states out of which the nation has made itself, and sometimes even by an effort to raise the dialects of these provinces up to the literary standard of the national language. In this there is no disloyalty to the national ideal,—rather is it to be taken as a tribute to the nation, since it seeks to call attention again to the several strands twined in the single bond. In literature this tendency is reflected in a wider liking for local color and in an intenser relish for the flavor of the soil. We find Verga painting the violent passions of the

Sicilians, and Reuter depicting the calmer joys of the Platt-Deutsch. We see Maupassant etching the canny and cautious Normans, while Daudet brushed in broadly the expansive exuberance of the Provençals. We delight alike in the Wessex-folk of Mr. Hardy and in the humorous Scots of Mr. Barrie. We extend an equal welcome to the patient figures of New England spinsterhood as drawn by Miss Jewett and Miss Wilkins, and to the virile Westerners set boldly on their feet by Mr. Wister and Mr. Garland.

What we wish to have explored for us are not only the nooks and corners of our own nation; those of other races appeal also to our sympathetic curiosity. These inquiries help us to understand the larger peoples, of whom the smaller communities are constituent elements. They serve to sharpen our insight into the differences which divide one race from another; and the contrast of Daudet and Maupassant on the one hand with Mark Twain and Kipling on the other brings out the width of the gap that yawns between the Latins (with their solidarity of the family and their reliance on the social instinct) and the Teutons (with their energetic independence and their aggressive individuality). With increase of knowledge there is less likelihood of mutual misunderstandings; and here literature performs a most useful service to the cause of civilization.

As Tennyson once said: "It is the authors, more than the diplomats, who make nations love one another." Fortunately, no high tariff can keep out the masterpieces of foreign literature which freely cross the frontier, bearing messages of good-will and broadening our understanding of our fellowmen.

IV

THE deeper interest in the expression of national qualities and in the representation of provincial peculiarities is to-day accompanied by an increasing cosmopolitanism which seems to be casting down the barriers of race and of language. More than fourscore years ago, Goethe said that even then national literature was "rather an unmeaning term" as "the epoch of world-literature was at hand." With all his wisdom Goethe failed to perceive that cosmopolitanism is a sorry thing when it is not the final expression of patriotism. An artist without a country and with no roots in the soil of his nativity is not likely to bring forth flower and fruit. As an American critic aptly put it, "a true cosmopolitan is at home,—even in his own country." A Russian novelist set forth the same thought; and it was the wisest character in Turgenieff's 'Dimitri Roudine' who asserted that the great misfortune of the hero was his ignorance of his native land:—" Russia can get along without any of us, but we cannot do without Russia. Wo betide him who does not understand her, and still more him who really forgets the manners and the ideas of his fatherland! Cosmopolitanism is an absurdity and a zero,—less than a zero; outside of nationality, there is no art, no truth, no life possible."

Perhaps it may be feasible to attempt a reconciliation of Turgenieff and Goethe, by pointing out that the cosmopolitanism of this growing century is revealed mainly in a similarity of the external forms of literature, while it is the national spirit which supplies the essential inspiration that gives life. For example, it is a fact that the 'Demi-monde' of Dumas, the 'Pillars of Society' of Ibsen, the 'Magda' of Sudermann, the 'Grand Galeoto' of Echegaray, the 'Second Mrs. Tanqueray' of Pinero, the 'Gioconda' of d'Annunzio are all of them cast in the same dramatic mold; but it is also a fact that the metal of which each is made was smelted in the native land of its author. Similar as they are in structure, in their artistic formula, they are radically dissimilar in their essence, in the motives that move the characters and in their outlook on life; and this dissimilarity is due not alone to the individuality of the several authors,—it is to be credited chiefly to the nationality of each.

Of course, international borrowings have always been profitable to the arts,—not merely the taking over of raw material, but the more stimulating absorption of methods and processes and even of artistic ideals. The Sicilian Gorgias had for a pupil the Attic Isocrates; and the style of the Athenian was imitated by the Roman Cicero, thus helping to sustain the standard of oratory in every modern language. The 'Matron of Ephesus' of Petronius was the great-grandmother of the 'Yvette' of Maupassant; and the dialogs of Herondas and of Theocritus serve as models for many a vignette of modern life. The 'Golden Ass' went before 'Gil Blas' and made a path for him; and 'Gil Blas' pointed the way for 'Huckleberry Finn.' It is easy to detect the influence of Richardson on Rousseau, of Rousseau on George Sand, of George Sand on Turgenieff, of Turgenieff on Mr. Henry James, of Mr. James on M. Paul Bourget, of M. Bourget on Signor d'Annunzio; and yet there is no denying that Richardson is radically English, that Turgenieff is thoroly Russian, and that d'Annunzio is unquestionably Italian.

In like manner we may recognize the striking similarity—but only in so far as the external form is concerned—discoverable in those short-stories which are as abundant as they are important in every modern literature; and yet much of our delight in these brief studies from life is due to the pungency of their local flavor, whether they were written by Kjelland or by Sacher-Masoch, by Auerbach or by Daudet, by Barrie or by Bret Harte. "All can grow the flower now, for all have got the seed"; but the blossoms are rich with the strength of the soil in which each of them is rooted.

This racial individuality is our immediate hope; it is our safeguard against mere craftsmanship, against dilettant dexterity, against cleverness for its own sake, against the danger that our cosmopolitanism may degenerate into Alexandrianism and that our century may come to be like the age of the Antonines, when a "cloud of critics, of compilers, of commentators darkened the face of learning," so Gibbon tells us, and "the decline of genius was soon followed by the corruption of taste." It is the spirit of nationality which will help to supply needful idealism. It will allow a man of letters to frequent the past without becoming archaic and to travel abroad without becoming exotic, because it will supply him always with a good reason for remaining a citizen of his own country.

(1904.)

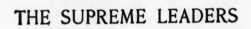

THE SUPREME LEADERS

THE SUPREME LEADERS

IN the fading annals of French Romanticism it
is recorded that at the first performance of
an early play of the elder Dumas at the Odéon,
a band of enthusiasts, as misguided as they were
youthful, were so completely carried away that
they formed a ring and danced in derision around
a bust of Racine which adorned that theater, declaring boisterously that the elder dramatist was
disgraced and disestablished: ' *Enfoncé Racine !* '

This puerile exploit took place not fourscore
years ago, and already has this play of Dumas
disappeared beneath the wave of oblivion, its
very name being recalled only by special students
of the history of the French stage, while the
Comédie-Française continues, year in and year
out, to act the best of Racine's tragedies, now
nearly two centuries and a half since they were
first performed.

Again, in the records of the British theater of
the eighteenth century, we find mention of a
countryman of John Home, who attended the
first performance of the reverend author's ' Doug-

las.' The play so worked upon the feelings of
this perfervid Scot that he was forced to cry out
triumphantly: "Whaur 's your Wully Shakspere
noo?"

And yet this Scottish masterpiece failed to
establish itself finally on the stage; and it has
long since past out of men's memories, leaving
behind it only a quotation or two and a speech
for boys to spout.   So in every age the disinterested observer can take note of the rise and fall
of some unlucky author or artist, painter or poet,
widely and loudly proclaimed as a genius, only
to be soon forgotten, often in his own generation.   He may have soared aloft for a brief moment with starry scintillations, like a rocket, only
at last to come down like the stick, empty and
unnoticed.

The echoes of the old battle of the Ancients
and Moderns have not died away, even yet; and
there is never a time when some ardent disciple
is not insisting that his immediate master must
be admitted as one of the immortals, and when
some shrill youth is not ready to make room for
the new-comer by ousting any number of the
consecrated chiefs of art.   Now and again, of
course, the claim is allowed; the late arrival is
made welcome in the Pantheon; and there is a
new planet on high.   But most of those who
are urged for this celestial promotion prove to

be mere shooting-stars at best, vanishing into space before there is opportunity to examine their spectrum and to compare it with that of the older orbs which have made the sky glorious thru the long centuries.

It is only by comparison with these fixt stars that we can measure the light of any new luminary which aspires to their lofty elevation. It is only by keeping our gaze full upon them that we may hope to come to an understanding of their immeasurable preëminence. Taine has told us that " there are four men in the world of art and of literature exalted above all others, and to such a degree as to seem to belong to another race— namely, Dante, Shakspere, Beethoven, and Michelangelo. No profound knowledge, no full possession of all the resources of art, no fertility of imagination, no originality of intellect, sufficed to secure them this position, for these they all had. These, moreover, are of secondary importance; that which elevated them to this rank is their soul."

Here we have four great lights for us to steer by when we are storm-driven on the changing sea of contemporary opinion and contemporary prejudice; and by their aid we may hope to win safety in a harbor of refuge.

Perhaps it is a praiseworthy striving for a permanent standard of value which accounts for the many attempts to draw up lists of the Hundred Best Books and of the Hundred Best Pictures. It may be admitted at once that these lists, however inadequate they must be, and however unsatisfactory in themselves, may have a humble utility of their own as a first aid to the ignorant. At least, they may serve to remind a man lost in a maze amid the clatter and the clutter of our own time, that after all this century of ours is the heir of the ages, and that it is for us to profit by the best that the past has bequeathed to us. Even the most expertly selected list could do little more than this.

Nevertheless these attempts, after all, cannot fail to be more or less misleading, since the best books and the best pictures do not number exactly a hundred. Nor can there be any assured certainty in the selection, since no two of those most competent to make the choice would be likely to agree on more than half of the masterpieces they would include.

The final and fatal defect in all these lists is that they seek to single out an arbitrary number of works of the highest distinction, instead of trying to find out the few men of supreme genius who were actually the makers of acknowledged masterpieces. It is of no consequence whether we hold that 'Hamlet' or 'Macbeth' is the most splendid example of Shakspere's surpassing endowment, or whether we consider the 'Fourth Symphony' or the 'Seventh' the completest expression of Beethoven's mastery of mus'c. What it is of consequence for us to recognize and to grasp effectually is that Shakspere and Beethoven are two of the indisputable chiefs, each in his own sphere. What it imports us to realize is that there is in every art a little group of supreme leaders ; they may be two or three only; they may be half a dozen, or, at the most, half a score; but they stand in the forefront, and their supremacy is inexpugnable for all time.

Every one recognizes to-day that "certain poets like Dante and Shakspere, certain composers like Beethoven and Mozart, hold the foremost place in their art." So Taine insisted, adding that this foremost place is also "accorded to Goethe, among the writers of our century; to Rembrandt among the Dutch painters; to Titian among the Venetians." And then Taine asserted also that "three artists of the Italian renascence, Leonardo da Vinci, Michelangelo, and Raphael, rise, by unanimous consent, far above all others."

No doubt this list of supreme leaders in the arts is unduly scanted; but there is wisdom in Taine's parsimony of praise. The great names he has here selected for signal eulogy are those whose appeal is universal and whose fame far transcends the boundaries of any single race.

It may have been from Sainte-Beuve that Taine inherited his catholicity of taste and his elevation of judgment; and it was due to the influence of Sainte-Beuve also that Matthew Arnold attained to a breadth of vision denied to most other British critics. Arnold invited us to "conceive of the whole group of civilized nations as being, for intellectual and spiritual purposes, one great confederation whose members have a due knowledge both of the past out of which they all proceed, and of one another." He went on to suggest that for any artist or poet "to be recognized by the verdict of such a confederation as a master is indeed glory, a glory which it would be difficult to rate too highly. For what could be more beneficent, more salutary? The world is forwarded by having its attention fixt on the best things; and here is a tribunal, free from all suspicion of national and provincial partiality, putting a stamp on the best things and recommending them for general honor and acceptance." Then he added the shrewd suggestion that there would be direct advantage to each race in seeing which of its own great men had been promoted to the little group of supreme leaders, since "a nation is furthered by recognition of its real gifts and successes; it is encouraged to develop them further."

Who, then, are the supreme leaders in the

several departments of human endeavor? By common consent of mankind who are the supreme soldiers, the supreme painters, the supreme poets? To attempt to name them is as difficult as it is dangerous; but the effort itself may be profitable, even if the ultimate result is not wholly satisfactory. To undertake this is not to revive the puerile debate as to whether Washington or Napoleon was the greater man; rather it is a frank admission that both were preëminent, with the further inquiry as to those others who may have achieved a supremacy commensurate with theirs. To seek out these indisputable masters is not to imitate the vain desire of the pedagog to give marks to the several geniuses, and to grade the greatest of men as if they were school-boys. There is no pedantry in striving to ascertain the list of the lonely few whom the assembled nations are all willing now to greet as the assured masters of the several arts.

The selection made by a single race or by a single century is not likely to be widely or permanently acceptable. Long years ago the Italians were wont to speak of the Four Poets, *quattro poete*, meaning thereby Dante, Petrarch, Ariosto, and Tasso. But this was a choice far too local and far too narrow. Of these four Italian poets perhaps only the severe Florentine has won his way outside of the boundaries of the language he

35

did so much to ennoble,—altho it may be admitted that the gentle Petrarch had also for a century a wide influence on the lyrists of other tongues.

Lowell had a more cosmopolitan outlook on literature, when he discust 'The Five Indispensable Authors'—Homer, Dante, Cervantes, Shakspere, and Goethe. "Their universal and perennial application to our consciousness and our experience accounts for their permanence and insures their immortality." We may admit that all five of the authors designated by Lowell are truly indispensable, just as we must accept also the incomparable position of the four leaders in the several arts whom Taine set apart in lonely elevation. But both Taine's list and Lowell's we feel to be too brief. The French critic had ranged thru every realm of art to discover finally that the incontestable masters were four and four only. The American critic, altho he limited himself to the single art of literature, dealt with it at large, not distinguishing between the poets and the masters of prose.

If we strike out of Lowell's list the single name of Cervantes, who was a poet only in a special and arbitrary sense, we shall have left the names of the four poets whose fame is world-wide— Homer, Dante, Shakspere, Goethe—the only poets whose supremacy is admitted thruout our modern civilization

To these Matthew Arnold insisted on adjoining a fifth, Milton; and we who speak the same tongue would gladly enroll the blind singer with the other four. Indeed, we might even hold Milton to be securer in this place than Goethe, who has not yet been a hundred years in his grave. But if we ask the verdict of "the whole group of civilized nations," which Matthew Arnold himself impaneled as "free from all suspicion of national and provincial partiality," we are met with the doubt whether Milton has established himself among the races that inherit the Latin tradition as securely as Dante has been accepted by the peoples of Teutonic stock. However high our own appreciation of Milton may be, the cosmopolitan verdict might not include him among the supreme poets. Indeed, we may doubt whether Vergil might not have more votes than Milton, when the struck jury is polled.

Here, perhaps, we may find our profit in applying a test suggested by Lowell—the test of imitability. "No poet of the first class has ever left a school, because his imagination is incommunicable," whereas "the secondary intellect seeks for excitement in expression, and stimulates itself into mannerism." The greater geniuses may have influenced those who came after them by their thoughts, by what they have contributed to the sum of human knowledge; but "they have not infected contemporaries or followers with mannerism." Then Lowell points out that "Dante, Shakspere, and Goethe, left no heirs either to the form or mode of their expression."

It was in his lecture on Emerson that Matthew Arnold asked: "Who are the great men of letters?"—meaning thereby the masters of prose. "They are men like Cicero, Plato, Bacon, Pascal, Swift, Voltaire—writers with, in the first place, a genius and instinct for style, writers whose prose is by a kind of native necessity true and sound." The British critic added that: "It is a curious thing, that quality of style, which marks the great writer, the born man of letters. It resides in the whole tissue of his work, and of his work regarded as a composition for literary purposes." The six masters of prose whom Arnold chose have all of them this quality of style; and their prose is true and sound. Altho this list of six was selected by an Englishman, and altho it contains the names of two Englishmen, it would be acceptable, one may venture to believe, to the cosmopolitan tribunal, to the heirs of the Latin tradition and to the peoples of the Teutonic stock. It may lack the completeness and the finality of the limitation of the supreme poets to four; but it must be taken as a not unsuccessful attempt to select the supreme prose-writers.

Arnold excluded Emerson from the class of "great men of letters" because the American philosopher had not the instinct for style, and because his prose was not always true and sound. Lowell, in a letter to a friend, protested against this, suggesting that the Oxford critic was like Renan in that he was apt to think "the *super*fine as good as the fine, or better even than that." Yet we may agree with the lecturer in holding that Emerson was rather to be ranked with Marcus Aurelius as "the friend of those who would live in the spirit," than to be classed with Cicero and with Swift, obviously inferior in elevation and in aim, but both of them born men of letters.

In like manner we must strike out the name of Burke from among the great orators. A political philosopher he was of keenest insight and of unfailing eloquence; but he was a poor speaker, and he did not often rivet the attention of the audiences he addrest. This is why he cannot establish a claim to inclusion among the supreme orators. Perhaps such a claim could be made good before the cosmopolitan tribunal by two speakers only, both belonging far back in the history of our civilization—Demosthenes and Cicero. Both revealed the needful double qualifications of the real orator, who shall hold his hearers in the hollow of his hand while he is speaking, bending them to his will and swaying them to the course he advocates, while the words he spoke then must survive now for our delight in their style and in their substance, a delight independent of the occasion of their utterance.

Others there are, no doubt, who were also possest of this double gift. The French, for instance, might well urge the claim of Bossuet to be raised to the same pinnacle; but the English and the Germans have not yielded to the spell of his majestic periods. Perhaps we here in the United States should not be extravagant if we set up also a claim for Daniel Webster; but, however firm our faith, and however solid our justification, we should be met with a silent stare from the French and the Italians and the Spaniards, who might fail even to recognize Webster's name. Demosthenes and Cicero alone would be hailed as the supreme orators thruout the whole group of civilized nations.

There is close kinship between oratory and history; and as the supreme orators are only two, one a Greek and the other a Roman, so the supreme historians, however tightly we may restrict the selection, will include a Greek, Thucydides, and a Roman, Tacitus. With them, and not inferior, stands Gibbon; and perhaps these three, Thucydides, Tacitus, and Gibbon, are all about whom there would be nowhere any dispute. But there is need to note that Taine held

Macaulay to be in no wise inferior to Gibbon. Again, it may be well to mention also that an American authority insists on elevating Voltaire also, as the earliest of the modern masters of history.

So we find that the supreme historians are three at the least, and at most four or five, just as the supreme poets are four, the supreme masters of prose are perhaps six, and the supreme orators are only two. And if we apply the same standards, if we disregard personal and provincial and national predilections and preferences, if we try to take the verdict of the cosmopolitan tribunal, we should find that the supreme dramatists are but three—Sophocles, Shakspere, and Molière. These three only were at once playwrights of contemporary popularity, masters of dramaturgic craftsmanship, creators of character independent of their own personality, makers of plays which deal with themes of an import at once permanent and universal, and poets also, each with his own philosophy of life.

Others there are who unite some of these qualifications, but none who can make good a right to be ranked with the mighty three. It is true that the power of Æschylus is as undeniable as the pathos of Euripides; but it is always the clear-eyed Sophocles whom Aristotle accepted as the master of all who strive for distinction in the theater. And Aristophanes, with all his exuberance of humor and all his lyric elevation, is, after all, too local and too temporary to be ranked with the broad-minded Molière. So also Calderon, whom the polemic Schlegel wisht to promote to an equality with the very greatest of dramatic poets, is too careless of form and too medieval in spirit. Promotion must also be denied, for one reason or another, to Ben Jonson, to Corneille and Racine, to Schiller, to Alfieri, and to Victor Hugo. However ardently their claims may be urged by their compatriots, the international tribunal would refuse to admit any one of them to an equality with Sophocles, Shakspere, and Molière, the greatest of the Greeks, the greatest of the English, the greatest of the French, the three races that have excelled in the arts of the theater.

Even tho no German can sustain a claim to supremacy in the drama, it is to the Germans that the consent of the whole world now awards the incontestable supremacy in the sister art of music. To the race that gave birth to Bach and Beethoven, to Mozart and Schubert and Wagner, it matters little whether the chiefs of music number two only, or whether they may be so many as four or five. Indeed, it may be admitted at once that the list would need to be widely extended before it would include the name of any composer who was not a scion of the Teutonic stock.

There is a certain significance, also, in the

probability that the outsider who could best jus-
tify a claim for inclusion would be a Russian
rather than an Italian or a Frenchman. And this
estimate, it may be well to confess, is not personal to the present writer, who has no skill in
music and scant acquaintance with its intricacies;
it is the outcome of a disinterested endeavor to
discover the consensus of expert opinion, free
from any racial bias.

But the northern races who excel in the art of
the musician seem to be inferior to the southern
in the arts of the painter and of the sculptor,—
more particularly in the latter. The supreme
sculptors are apparently two or three: Phidias
and Michelangelo, beyond all question, and with
them probably we ought also to place Donatello.
Of Praxiteles we know too little. Of most other
artists in marble and in bronze we know too
much, however fine their occasional achievements,—Verrocchio's ' Colleoni,' for example.
They do not sustain themselves at the lofty level
on which Michelangelo moves with certainty
and ease—"the greatest of known artists," so
Mr. Lafarge has ventured to acclaim him; and
just as Shakspere is unsurpassed as a poet and
also as a playwright, just as Cicero takes a foremost
place as an orator and also as a writer of prose,
so Michelangelo is mighty as a sculptor, as an
architect, and as a painter.

As a painter he has more rivals than as a

sculptor. We may limit the supreme masters of the plastic art to two, or to three at the most; but the supreme masters of the pictorial art are twice three, at the very least. By tne side of Michelangelo there is Raphael, also an Italian; and has any one really a right to exclude Titian from their fellowship? Then there are Velasquez, the Spaniard, and Dürer, the German. And farther north in the Netherlands, there are Rembrandt and Rubens; and ought not Vandyke to be allowed to stand aloft with them ? Six, at the lowest count, and eight by the more liberal estimate, are the men who have gone to the forefront in the art of the brush, half of them from the north and half of them from the south; and among them all not one who had English for his native speech, and not one whose mother-tongue was French. Indeed, at least one German, Holbein, and two or three more Italians would be admitted within the sacred enclosure before any Frenchman or any Englishman could have free entry.

Those who speak French and those who speak English fare no better when we turn from the arts of peace to the art of war. Every race takes pride in the renown of the far-sighted and swift-striking commanders who have led it to victory, and every race is prone to over-estimate the military genius of its own successful soldiers. Here

44

in the United States we seek to set up Washington and Grant and Lee as the rivals of the most gifted warriors that the old world has to show in all the long centuries of its incessant warfare; and in Great Britain our kin across the sea are led by local loyalty to do the same disservice to Marlborough and Wellington.   But if we were to search the countless treatises on battles and campaigns written in every modern language, we should soon be forced to record that there were five men, and only five, whom the experts of every race united in singling out.   In any list of the ten greatest soldiers, prepared in any country in the world, these five names would surely appear, even tho the other names on the several lists might be those of merely national heroes.   The five international masters of war are Alexander, Hannibal, Cæsar, Frederick, and Napoleon.

Napoleon, altho he rose to be Emperor of the French, was a Corsican by birth and an Italian by descent.   The French have ever battled bravely for military glory; but they have not brought forth one of the supreme soldiers.   The race that speaks English has done its full share of fighting on land and on sea, but it is on the blue water that it can give the best account of itself.   The supreme leaders in war at sea worthy to be set by the side of the five supreme leaders in war on land are two at the very utmost; and probably an international tribunal would hold that Nelson alone was to be classed with Alexander, Hannible, Cæsar, Frederick, and Napoleon. But it is the opinion of the foremost living expert on sea-power that Farragut deserves to be placed not far distant from Nelson, and that the gap which separates the American sailor from the British is smaller than that which stretches between Farragut and the third claimant, whoever he may be and of whatever nationality.

Turning from the art of war and from the arts of peace to the sciences whereon all the arts are based, we find that the English and the French are richly represented. The supreme leaders in science, the men whose discoveries have been fecundating and fundamental, seem to be at least seven—Euclid, Archimedes, Copernicus, Newton, Laplace, Lavoisier, and Darwin. This list might well be larger; it could not be less; and no matter how it might be extended it would include these seven. None of them was merely an inventor of specific devices; all of them were discoverers of essential principles, and thereby contributors to the advancement of civilization and to man's mastery of knowledge.

It would be interesting, as it would be instructive, if we could also enumerate the supreme leaders in religion; but this is a field in which prejudice is too violent ever to permit a serene view, and there is no hoping for an international verdict. Nor would it be possible to find any agreement as to the supreme statesmen, leaders of men and makers of nations. That Washington could not be excluded from any choice, however limited, we may rest assured; but who or how many might really deserve to be set beside him, we can only guess. National pride is as potent as religious feeling, and there is no likelihood that rival patriotisms can ever be reconciled.

A comparison of the several lists will serve to show the field in which each of the great races of the world has revealed its native qualities; and, as Matthew Arnold suggested, this is most useful, since a nation is benefitted " by recognition of its real gifts and successes; it is encouraged to develop them further. '

And a consideration also of the character of each of the men whose names have here been set on high as the supreme leaders of humanity will make clear once more what is often clouded and obscured—the fact that the true genius is never an erratic creature, irregular and irresponsible, clamoring for indulgence and appealing for pity. He is always strong and sane and wholesome. Clear-eyed and broad-minded, he has self-control and common-sense.

(1905.)

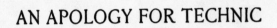

AN APOLOGY FOR TECHNIC

AN APOLOGY FOR TECHNIC

I F the chief end of all art is delight, there is small blame to be attached to most of us in that we are glad to take our pleasure carelessly and to give little thought to the means whereby we have been moved. Properly enough, the enjoyment of most of us is unthinking; and in the appreciation of the masterpieces of the several arts few of us are wont to consider curiously the craftsmanship of the men who wrought these marvels, their skill of hand, their familiarity with the mechanics of their art, their consummate knowledge of technic. Our regard is centered rather on the larger aspects of the masterwork, on its meaning and on its veracity, on its intellectual elevation, and on its moral appeal. No doubt this is best, for it is only by its possession of these nobler qualities that a work of art endures. On the other hand, these nobler qualities by themselves will not suffice to confer immortality, unless they are sustained by the devices of the adroit craftsman. As Massinger asserted long ago:

No fair colors
Can fortify a building faintly joined.

Technic is most successful when its existence is least suspected, and this is one reason why it is often overlooked and neglected in the very achievements which owe to its aid their vitality. Perhaps this happens the more frequently because it is the affectation of many an artist to hurry his tools out of sight as swiftly as he can, and to sweep up the chips of his workshop as soon as may be, so that the result of his effort shall seem almost as if it were the sudden effect of the inspiration that is believed to visit a genius now and again. He may have toiled at it unceasingly for months, joying in the labor and finding keen pleasure in every workmanlike artifice he had used to attain his end; and yet he refrains from confessing his many struggles with his rebellious material, wisely preferring to let what he has done speak for itself, simply and without commentary. But the artists know that the pathway to achievement is never along the line of least resistance; and they smile when they hear Mascarille, in Molière's little comedy, tell the affected young ladies whom he is seeking to impress that all he did "was done without effort." By this the artists at once perceive the fellow to be a pretender, who had never accomplished anything and who never would. They know, as no others can know, that there is no cable-road to the tops of the twin-peaks of Parnassus, and that he who would climb to these remote heights must trudge afoot, —even if he is lucky enough now and again to get a lift on Pegasus.

What the artists do not care to parade, it is the duty of the commentators to point out; and an understanding of the technic of any art, of its possibilities and of its limitations, is as necessary for the critics as for the creators. Perhaps it is not pedantic to suggest that the critic who seeks to be of service ought to be able to see in every masterpiece the result of the combined action of three forces, without any one of which that work of art could not have come into being. First, there is the temperament of the artist himself, his native endowment for the practise of that special art, his gift of story-telling or of play-making, as the case may be. Second, there is the training of the artist, his preparation for his work, his slowly acquired mastery of the processes of his craft, his technical accomplishments. And, thirdly, there is the man's own character, his intelligence, and energy, and determination, his moral sense, his attitude toward life and its insistent problems. Now, of these three necessary factors—first, his native gift; second, his technic; and, third, his character—

only the second is improvable by taking thought. The native gift must remain ever what it is, neither more nor less; and it cannot be enlarged by any effort of will. So also the character, which is conditioned by much that is beyond a man's control, — which can be bettered, perhaps, but only as the man himself climbs upward.

Technic, however, can be had for the asking. Any man can acquire it if he will but pay the price, — the needful study and experiment. Any man can make himself a master of his craft, if he will but serve his apprenticeship loyally. The beginner in painting, for example, can go into the studio of an older practitioner to get grounded in the grammar of his art, and to learn slowly how to speak its language, not eloquently at first, but so as to make his meaning clear. In that workshop he soon awakens to the fact that permanent success is never won by any audacity of ignorance, and that the most famous artists are those who acquainted themselves with every artifice of their craft and with every trick of their trade. They went to school to certain of their elders to acquire that tradition of technic, past along from hand to hand, enriched by the devices of one after another of the strong men who had practised the art, following each in the other's footsteps and broadening the trail blazed by those who went first.

Every generation is privileged to stand on the shoulders of its predecessors, and it is taller by what they accomplished. The art of fiction, for example, is a finer art to-day than it was yester-day; and so is every other art, even tho the artists themselves are no greater now than then, and even tho genius is no more frequent than it was formerly. Ghirlandajo and Marlowe and Cervantes were men of genius; but their technic is seen to-day to be as primitive as their native talent is indisputable. We can perceive them doubtfully feeling for a formula, fumbling in the dark, for want of the model which they them-selves were to aid in establishing and which every novice nowadays has ready to his hand, even tho he may lack the temperament to profit by what is set before him.

It is significant that not a few of the masters, in the days when they were but novices, found so much satisfaction in this mere acquiring of the secrets of the craft, that they chose to linger in the apprentice-stage longer than might seem necessary. In their earlier work they were con-tent modestly to put in practise the technical principles they had just been acquiring; and for a little while they sought scarcely more than mere technical adroitness. Consider the firstlings of Shakspere's art and of Molière' ; and observe how they reveal these prentice playwrights at work, each seeking to display his cleverness and each satisfied when he had done this. In 'Love's Labor 's Lost,' Shakspere is trying to amuse by inventive wit and youthful gaiety and ingenuity of device, just as Molière in the 'Étourdi' is enjoying his own complicating of comic imbroglios, not yet having anything of importance to say on the stage, but practising against the time when he should want to say something. Neither in the English comedy nor in the French is there any purpose other than the desire to please by the devices of the theater.

There is so little hint of a deeper meaning in either 'Love's Labor 's Lost' or the 'Étourdi,' of a moral, so to speak, of a message of ulterior significance, that, if Shakspere and Molière had died after these plays were produced, nobody would ever have suspected that either youthful playwright had it in him to develop into a philosophic observer of the deeper realities of life. Of course, neither of them was long satisfied with this dexterous display of technical adroitness alone; and, as they grew in years, we find their plays getting richer in meaning and dealing more seriously with the larger problems of existence. But technic was never despised; and, if it was not always the chief end of the playwright, it remained the means whereby he was enabled to erect the solid framework of masterpieces like

'Othello' and 'Tartuffe,' in which the crafts-manship is overshadowed by the nobler qualities, no doubt, but in which the stark technical skill is really more abundant than in the earlier and emp-tier plays.

As Shakspere and Molière matured mentally and morally, so also did they grow in facility of accomplishment, in the ease with which they could handle the ever-present problems of expo-sition and construction. The student of drama-turgy notes with increasing delight the inge-nuity with which the first appearance of Tar-tuffe is prepared; and he finds an almost equal joy in the bolder beginnings of 'Romeo and Ju-liet' and of 'Hamlet,' where the difficulty was less, it may be, but where the interest of the craftsman in the excellence of his device is quite as obvious. Shakspere was the greatest of dra-matic poets and Molière was the greatest of comic dramatists; and both of them were good work-men, taking an honest pride in the neatness with which they finished a job. In his later years, Shakspere seems to have relaxed a little his in-terest in technic, and the value of his work is at once seen to suffer. Altho his mind is as pow-erful as ever up to the last years of his stay in London, 'Cymbeline' and 'A Winter's Tale' are far inferior to 'Hamlet' and to 'Macbeth'; and the cause is apparently little more than a carelessness of technic, an unwillingness to take the trouble needful to master his material and to present it in due proportion.

If Shakspere and Molière ever meet in that other world which was so much in the mind of the one and so little in the thought of the other, and if they chance to fall into chat—Shakspere spoke French, pretty certainly, even if Molière knew no English—we may rest assured that they will not surprize each other by idle questions about the meaning of this play or that, its moral purpose or its symbolic significance. We may be confident that their talk would turn promptly to technic; and, perhaps, Shakspere would congratulate Molière on his advantage in coming later, when the half-open, semi-medieval playhouse, with which the English dramatist had perforce to be contented, had been superseded by a more modern theater, roofed and lighted and set with scenery. And, in his turn, Molière might be curious to inquire how the English playwright was able to produce upon the spectators the effect of a change of scene when, in fact, there was no actual scenery to change.

To suggest that these two masters of the dramatic art would probably confine their conversation to matters of mere technic is not so vain or adventurous as it may seem, since technic is the one theme the dramatists from Lope de

Vega to Legouvé have always chosen to discuss, whenever they have been emboldened to talk about their art in public. Lope's 'New Art of Writing Plays' is in verse, and it has taken for its remote model Horace's 'Art of Poetry,' but none the less does it contain the practical counsels of a practical playwright, advising his fellow-craftsmen how best to succeed on the stage; and it is just as technical in its precepts as Mr. Pinero's acute lecture on the probable success of Robert Louis Stevenson as a dramatist, if only the Scots romancer had taken the trouble to learn the rules of the game, as it is played in the theater of to-day.

In thus centering the interest of their public utterance upon the necessities of craftsmanship, the dramatists are in accord with the customs of the practitioners of all the other arts. Consider the criticism of poetry by the poets themselves, for example,—how narrowly it is limited to questions of vocabulary or of versification, whether the poet-critic is Dryden or Wordsworth or Poe. Consider the criticism of painting by the painters themselves,—how frankly it is concerned with the processes of the art, whether the painter-critic is Fromentin or La Farge. It is La Farge who records that Rembrandt was a "workman following his trade of painting to live by it," and who reminds us that "these very great artists"—

Rembrandt and his fellows—"are primarily workmen, without any pose or assumption of doing more than a daily task." What they did was all in the day's work. One of the most distinguished of American sculptors was once standing before a photograph of the Panathenaic frieze, and a critical friend by his side exprest a wonder as to "what those old Greeks were thinking of when they did work like that?" The professional artist smiled and responded: "I guess that, like the rest of us, they were thinking how they could pull it off!"

The method, the tricks of the trade, the ingenious devices of one kind or another, these are what artists of all sorts like to discuss with fellow-practitioners of the art; and it is by this interchange of experiences that the means of expression are multiplied. The inner meaning of what they have wrought, its message, its morality, its subtler spirit, the artists do not care ever to talk over, even with each other. This is intangible and incommunicable; and it is too personal, too intimate, to be vulgarized in words; it is to be felt rather than phrased. Above all, it must speak for itself, for it is there because it had to be there, and not because the artist put it there deliberately. If he has not builded better than he knew, then is the result of his labor limited and narrow. A story is told of Thorwaldsen in his old age, when a friend found him disconsolate before a finished statue and inquired if he was despondent because he had not been able to realize his ideal. And the sculptor responded that, on the contrary, he had realized his ideal, and therefore he was downcast; for the first time his hand had been able to accomplish all that his mind had planned.

"Neither in life, nor even in literature and in art, can we always do what we intend to do," M. Brunetière once asserted, adding that, "in compensation, we have not always intended to do all that we have actually accomplished." Often no one is more astonished than the artist himself— be he poet or painter—at what the critics sometimes find in his work; and he is frankly unaware of any intention on his part to do all the fine things which he is told that he has done. But the critics may be justified, despite the disclaimer of the artist; and the fine things are, of a truth, to be discovered even tho they get into the work by accident, as it were, and even tho they may be the result of an intention which was either unconscious on the artist's part, or subconscious.

We cannot help feeling the sublimity so obvious in the frescos of the Sistine Chapel; and yet it is equally obvious—if we care to look for the evidence—that while he was at this work the mind of Michelangelo was absorbed by the conquest of a host of technical difficulties. Of course, it would be going too far to assert that the great artist did not actually intend the sublimity that we admire and wonder at; but we may be sure that this sublimity is not something deliberately planned and achieved by him. It is there because the theme evoked it, and because Michelangelo was himself a man of the noblest character and of the loftiest imagination. It was inherent and latent in him, and it had to come out, inevitably and mightily, when he was engaged on a piece of work that tasked all his powers.

An ideal, a significance, a moral, that has to be inserted into a work of art and that might have been omitted, is not likely to be firmly joined; and it is liable to fall apart sooner or later. Morality, for example, is not something to be put in or left out, at the caprice of the creator; it is, as Mr. Henry James once called it, "a part of the essential richness of inspiration." Therefore the artist need not give thought to it. If his own soul is as clean as may be, and if his vision is clear, the moral of his work may be left to take care of itself. Nearly always when an artist has been over-anxious to charge his work with a moral message, written so plain that all who run may read, he has failed to attain either of his ends, the ethical or the esthetic. There is a purpose plainly exprest in Miss Edgeworth's 'Moral Tales' and in her 'Parent's Assistant'; and the result is that healthy girls and wholesome boys are revolted. There was no moral intent in her ever-delightful 'Castle Rackrent'; and yet it has an ethical significance which few of its readers can have failed to feel.

Perhaps 'Castle Rackrent' is the finest of Miss Edgeworth's stories, because it is the only one in which she had set herself a technical problem of exceeding difficulty. She chose to use the faithful old retainer to tell the tale of the family's downfall in consequence of its weakness, its violence, and its vice. Thady has never a word of blame for any son of the house he has served generation after generation. Indeed, he is forever praising his succession of masters; but so artfully does the author utilize the device of transparency that the reader is put in possession of the damning facts, one by one, and is soon able to see the truth of the matter which Thady himself has no thought of revealing,—which, indeed, he would probably deny indignantly if it was suggested by any one else.

The chief reason why the novel is still held to be inferior to the drama is to be found in its looseness of form. The novel is not strictly limited, as the play must be by the practical necessities of the theater; and the practitioners of the art of fiction permit themselves a license of structure which cannot but be enfeebling to the artists themselves. Few of the novelists have ever gone about a whole winter with a knot in their foreheads, such as Hawthorne carried there while he was thinking out the 'Scarlet Letter.' And only by strenuous grappling with his obstacles was he able to attain the masterly simplicity of that Puritan tragedy. A resolute wrestling with difficulty is good not only for the muscles but also for the soul; and it may be because they know this, that artists are inclined to go afield in search of difficulties to be overthrown, that they set themselves problems, that they accept limitations. Herein we may see a cause for the long popularity of the sonnet, with its restricted scheme of rimes. Herein, again, we may see a reason for the desire of the novelist to try his fate as a dramatist. "To work successfully beneath a few grave, rigid laws," so Mr. James once declared, "is always a strong man's highest ideal of success." The novelist often fails as a dramatist, because he has the gift of the story-teller only, and not that of the play-maker, but more often still because the writing of fiction has provided him with no experience in working beneath any law other than his own caprice.

The modern sculptor, by the mere fact that he may now order marble of any shape and of any size, finds his work far easier and, therefore, far less invigorating than it was long ago, when the artist needed to have an alerter imagination to perceive in a given piece of marble the beautiful figure he had to cut out of that particular block and no other.   Professor Mahaffy has suggested that the decay of genius may be traced to the enfeebling facilities of our complex civilization.   " In art," he maintained, "it is often the conventional shackles,—the necessities of rime and meter, the triangle of a gable, the circular top of a barrel—which has led the poet, the sculptor, or the painter, to strike out the most original and perfect products of their art.   Obstacles, if they are extrinsic and not intrinsic, only help to feed the flame."   Professor Butcher has declared that genius "wins its most signal triumphs from the very limitations within which it works."   And this is what Gautier meant when he declared that the greater the difficulty the more beautiful the work; or, as Mr. Austin Dobson has paraphrased it:

> Yes; when the ways oppose—
> When the hard means rebel,
> Fairer the work outgrows,—
> More potent far the spell.

Not only has a useful addition to the accepted devices of the craft been the guerdon of a victorious grapple with a difficulty, but the successful effort to solve a purely technical problem has often led to an ennobling enlargement of the original suggestion, with which the artist might have rested content if he had not been forced to the struggle. From the history of sculpture and of architecture here in the United States during the last years of the nineteenth century, it is easy to select two instances of this enrichment of the fundamental idea, as the direct consequence of an unexpected obstacle which the artist refused to consider a stumbling-block, preferring to make it a stepping-stone to a loftier achievement.

When the city of New York was making ready to welcome the men of the navy on their return from Manila and Santiago, the Architectural League offered to design a triumphal arch. The site assigned, in front of Madison Square, just where Broadway slants across Fifth Avenue, forced the architect to face a difficulty seemingly unsurmountable. The line of march was to be along Fifth Avenue, and, therefore, the stately monument was set astride that street. But the line of approach, for most of the multitude certain to come to gaze on the temporary addition to civic beauty, was along Broadway; and the arch built squarely across the avenue would seem askew to all who first caught sight of it from the other street. To avoid this unfortunate effect the designer devised a colonnade, extending north and south, up and down the avenue. Thus he corrected the apparent slant by emphasizing the fact that it was the avenue in which the arch was placed and not the more popular highway that chanced to cut across it. But this colonnade, invented solely to solve a difficulty, lent itself readily to rich adornment. It became at once an integral element of the architectural scheme, to which it gave breadth as well as variety. It was accepted instantly as a welcome modification of the tradition,—as an amplification not to be wantonly disregarded by any architect hereafter called upon to design a triumphal arch.

To this illustration from architecture may be added another from sculpture, as suggestive and as useful in showing how a conquest of technical difficulty is likely ever to increase the resources of the art. The sculptor of the statue of Lincoln, which ennobles a park of Chicago, was instructed that the work of his hands was to stand upon a knoll, visible from all sides, stark against the sky, unprotected by any background of entablature or canopy. The gaunt figure of Lincoln is not a thing of beauty to be gazed at from all the points of the compass; and the stern veracity of the artist would not permit him to disguise the ill-fitting coat and trousers by any arbitrary draperies, mendaciously cloaking the

AN APOLOGY FOR TECHNIC

clothes which were intensely characteristic of the man to be modeled. To shield the awkwardness of the effigy when seen from the rear, a chair was placed behind it; and so the sculptor was led to present Lincoln as the Chief Magistrate of the Republic, arisen from the chair of state, to address the people from whom he had received his authority. And thus, at that late day, at the end of the nineteenth century, Mr. Saint-Gaudens did a new thing; altho there had been standing statues and seated statues, no sculptor had ever before designed a figure just rising from his seat.

It is by victories like these over technical difficulties that the arts advance; and it is in combats like these that the true artist finds his pleasure. The delight of battle is his, as he returns to the attack, again and again, until at last he wins the day and comes home laden with the spoil. The true artist hungers after technic for its own sake, well knowing the nourishment it affords. He even needlessly puts on fetters now and again, that he may find sharper zest in his effort. This ravenous appetite for technic leads many an artist to go outside his own art in search of unforeseen but fascinating difficulties. The painter is tempted to stretch his muscles by a tussle with the unknown obstacles of the sculptor; and the sculptor in his turn contends with the limitations of the painter. Michelangelo called himself a sculptor and pretended to

be no more; but in time he took up the craft of
the architect, of the painter and of the poet.
And this interchange of field in search of new
worlds to conquer seems to be characteristic of
the great periods of artistic activity and achievement. In all such periods, the more accomplished
craftsmen have never wearied of technical experiment to the constant enrichment of the processes of their art.

It is the uncreative critics, it is never the creative craftsmen, who dwell on the danger of
taking too much interest in technic. The critics
may think that the more attention the artist pays
to his manner, the less he has for his matter,
and that he is in peril of sacrificing content to
form. But the craftsmen themselves know better; they know that no one may surely separate
manner and matter, form and content, Siamese
twins often, coming into being at a single birth.
Furthermore, the artist knows that technic is the
one quality he can control, every man for himself, every man improving himself as best he can.
His native gift, his temperament,—this is what
it is; and what it is it must be; and no man
can better it by any effort. His character, also,
the personality of the artist, that which gives a
large meaning to his work,—how little can any
man control this result of heredity and environment?

If an artist has anything to say it will out,

sooner or later, however absorbed he may be in finding the best way of saying it. If he has nothing to say, if he has no message for the heart of man, he may at least give some pleasure to his contemporaries by the sheer dexterity of his craftsmanship. There would have been no more meaning in Poe's verse, if there had been less melody, if the poet had less devotedly studied the "book of iambs and pentameters." There would have been no larger significance in the painted epigrams of Gérôme, if that master of line had cared less for draftsmanship. There would have been no more solid value in the often amusing plays of Sardou, if he had not delighted in the ingenuity of his dramaturgical devices. At bottom, Sardou, Gérôme, and Poe, had little or nothing to say; that is their misfortune, no doubt; but it is not their fault, for, apparently, each one of them made the best of his native gift.

In his time Milton was the most careful and conscientious of artists in verse-making, and so, in his turn, was Pope, whose ideals were different, but whose skill was no less in its kind. So, again, was Tennyson untiring in seeking to attain ultimate perfection of phrase, consciously employing every artifice of alliteration, assonance and rime. But, if Milton's verse seems to us now noble and lofty, while Pope's appears to us as rather petty and merely clever, surely this is because Milton himself was noble and his native endowment lofty, and because Pope himself was petty and his gift only cleverness; surely it is not because they were both of them as much interested in the mechanics of their art as was Tennyson after them.

One of the wittiest critics of our modern civilization, the late Clarence King, remarked, some ten years ago, that the trouble with American fiction just then lay in the fact that it had the most elaborate machinery, —and no boiler. But the fault of our fiction at that time was to be sought in the absence of steam, —and not in the machinery itself which stood ready to do its work, to the best advantage and with the utmost economy of effort, just so soon as the power might be applied.

(1904.)

OLD FRIENDS WITH NEW FACES

OLD FRIENDS WITH NEW FACES

THACKERAY was frequent in praise of Fenimore Cooper, hailing Leatherstocking as better than any of "Scott's lot"; and this laudation appeared in the 'Roundabout Papers' long after the British novelist had paid to the American romancer the sincere flattery of borrowing from the last words of Natty Bumppo the suggestion, at least, of the last words of Colonel Newcome. Cooper's backwoodsman, hearing an inaudible roll-call had responded "Here!" a score of years before Thackeray's old soldier had become again a child to answer "Adsum!" Not less than a score of years later an old sailor in one of the stories of Sir Walter Besant made his final exit from this world with a kindred phrase, "Come on board, sir!" And then, once more, in one of Mr. Kipling's 'Plain Tales from the Hills,' we find the last dying speech and confession of a certain McIntosh who had been a scholar and a gentleman in days gone by, and who had sunk into irredeemable degradation in India. When his hour came, he rose in bed and said, as loudly as slowly, "Not guilty, my Lord!" Then he fell back, and the stupor held him till he died.

There are criticasters not a few who would denounce Thackeray and Besant and Mr. Kipling as arrant plagiarists; but critics of a more delicate perception of the principles of art would rather praise these authors for the ingenuity with which they had successively made use of Cooper's original device. Indeed, the more delicate the perceptions of the critic the less likely would he be to assert positively that all four authors had not hit on the same effect independently. Thackeray may have taken it over from Cooper, consciously or unconsciously; Besant may have borrowed it from either his British or his American predecessor; and Kipling may have been familiar with it in the pages of Cooper, of Thackeray, and of Besant, and still have found amusement in giving a new twist to an old trick. But it is perfectly possible that we have here an instance of purely accidental similarity, such as keen-eyed readers can discover abundantly in the highways and byways of literary history.

The theme of M. Paul Bourget's 'André Cornélis' is that of 'Hamlet,' but in all probability the French novelist was not aware that he was treading in the footsteps of the English dramatist until his own plot had taken shape in his mind.

A situation in 'Vanity Fair'—that of Dobbin in love with the widowed Amelia and yet unwilling to break down her belief in her dead husband's fidelity—was utilized in the 'Henrietta' of Mr. Bronson Howard, who was characteristically scrupulous in recording on the playbill his indebtedness to Thackeray's novel; and this same situation at about the same time had been utilized also in a little one-act play, 'This Picture and That,' by an author who had never doubted it to be of his own invention (altho he had read 'Vanity Fair' more than once), and who did not discover how he had exposed himself to the accusation of plagiarism until he happened to see the 'Henrietta' acted, and to perceive the full significance of Mr. Howard's memorandum.

It deserves to be noted also that when Colonel Esmond broke his sword before the unworthy prince whom he had served so long and so loyally, he was only following an example which had been set by the noble Athos, who had snapt his weapon asunder before Louis XIV because that inhuman monarch had taken for himself Mlle. de la Vallière, the young lady beloved by the Vicomte de Bragelonne, the son of Athos. And the same effect is to be found also in the opera of 'La Favorite.' The book of Donizetti's opera bears the names of Alphonse Royer and Gustave Vaëz; but it is said to have been revised by Scribe. It was derived from a forgotten play called the 'Comte de Comminges,' written by one Baculard-D'Arnaud, and this in turn had been taken from a novel written by the notorious Mme. de Tencin, the callous mother of D'Alembert. The scene of the sword-breaking is not in the novel or the play; and quite possibly it may have been introduced into the book of the opera by the fertile and ingenious Scribe. 'La Favorite' was produced in 1840, when Thackeray was in Paris preparing the 'Paris Sketch Book.' It was in 1850 that Dumas published the 'Vicomte de Bragelonne'; and it was in 1852 that Thackeray put forth 'Henry Esmond.' But it was back in 1829 that the commandant Hulot in Balzac's 'Chouans' had broken his sword across his knee rather than carry out an order that seemed to him unworthy. This is not quite the same effect that we find in 'La Favorite'; but none the less Scribe may have been indebted to Balzac for the suggestion.

There is no denying that the striking situation which Thackeray used with so much skill in his novel had already been utilized in the stirring romance of Dumas and in the pathetic libretto of Royer, Vaëz, and Scribe. Did Thackeray borrow it from the romance or from the libretto? Or did he reinvent it for himself, forgetting that it had already served? He was in Paris when

Donizetti's tuneful music was first heard; and he was going to the opera as often as he could. He was fond of Dumas's interminable tales of adventure; and he had a special liking for Athos. It is in one of the 'Roundabout Papers' —'On a Peal of Bells'—that he declared his preference. "Of your heroic heroes, I think our friend, Monseigneur Athos, Comte de la Fère, is my favorite." Is this a case of conveyance, such as is often carelessly called plagiarism? or is it a case of unconscious reminiscence? That Dumas knew what he was doing when he lifted the situation out of 'La Favorite' is very likely, for it was not his custom to be overscrupulous in taking what he could make his own. But Thackeray had been careful to credit the suggestion of one or two of his earlier French sketches to the Parisian story-tellers he had put under contribution. Besides he was a man of transparent honesty; and it is therefore highly probable that he had no consciousness that the scene was not original with him.

In one of his conversations with Eckermann, Goethe declared that Byron had not known how to meet the charge of levying on the earlier poets. The German sage asserted that the English bard should have been far bolder in his own defence, and far franker also. Byron should have said: "What is there, is mine; and whether I got it from a book or from life, is of no consequence; the only point is, whether I have made a right use of it." And then Goethe added that in one of the Waverley novels Scott had appropriated a scene from 'Egmont'; "and he had a right to do so; and because he did it well, he deserves praise." Goethe seemed to think that the privilege of using again what had been invented by another was justified only when the later author improved on the earlier, or at least attained to an equal level. He noted that Scott had taken Mignon in 'Wilhelm Meister' as the model of Fenella in 'Peveril of the Peak'—"but whether with equal judgment is another question."

Goethe was wise enough to know that human invention is finite and that the number of possible effects is limited. He once told Eckermann and Soret that the Italian playwright, Gozzi, had asserted the existence of only thirty-six possible tragic situations, and that Schiller had taken much trouble in trying to prove that there were more, only in the end to find himself unable to gather even so many as Gozzi had collected. "It is almost impossible, in the present day," commented Goethe, "to find a situation which is thoroly new. Only the manner of looking at it can be new, and the art of treating it and representing it."

Unfortunately, we have not Gozzi's list of the

three dozen situations, nor Schiller's smaller catalog to compare with it. Gérard de Nerval—that strangest figure of a strange period—considered the matter anew in the fervid days of French romanticism, and decided that there were in reality only twenty-four typical situations available for the theater; but his classification has also failed to come down to us. However, in the last decade of the nineteenth century an ingenious Frenchman, M. Georges Polti, accepting the number originally proposed by Gozzi, examined the plots of several thousand plays, classified the result of his arduous investigation, and published a little book of two hundred pages on the '36 Situations Dramatiques.'

Highly interesting as is M. Polti's book, there is not a little difficulty in grasping the theory upon which he has assorted his immense collection into exactly three dozen divisions. The logic of his grouping is not immediately apparent, as it would have been had he taken the passions, for instance, as the several foundations. His first situation, for example, is that which we find in one of the earliest of Greek plays, the 'Suppliants.' M. Polti entitles it 'To Implore,' and he indicates varying possible subdivisions: (AI) Fugitives imploring shelter against their enemies, as in the tragedy of Æschylus, the second act of Shakspere's 'King John,' and repeatedly in 'Uncle Tom's Cabin'; (B1) the ship-wrecked imploring hospitality, as in more than one ancient drama. But this first situation of his M. Polti finds to be infrequent on the modern stage, altho often met with in the Greek theater. His second situation, which we may call 'To Rescue from Imminent Danger,' has been widely popular alike with the ancients and the moderns, so we have in subdivision (A) a condemned person rescued by a hero, as in the myth of Andromeda, the folk-tale of Bluebeard, and the first act of 'Lohengrin'; and in subdivision (B2) a condemned person rescued by a guest of the house, as in the 'Alcestis' of Euripides.

These two situations, however, are far less effective in evoking the special pleasure proper to the theater than the nineteenth on M. Polti's list, "To kill unknowingly one of your own blood." The full force of the theatric effect of this situation is dependent on the spectators' complete knowledge of the relationship of slayer and slain, unsuspected by the victims themselves; and the strength of the situation resides not in the mere killing, which may indeed be averted at the last moment, but in the steadily gathering dread which ought to accompany the prepara-tions for the evil deed. This situation in one or another of its subdivisions we find in 'Nicholas Nickleby,' as well as in 'Œdipus the King' and in 'Lady Inger of Ostraat'; in Sophocles it is a son who murders his unknown father, and in Ibsen it is a mother who murders her unknown son. It is to be found in the 'Semiramis' of Voltaire, in the 'Merope' of Alfieri, in the 'Ion' of Euripides, and again and again in Victor Hugo's dramas. M. Polti points out that this single situation is utilized as the culminating point at the very end of four of Hugo's plays—the 'Burgraves,' 'Marie Tudor,' 'Lucrèce Borgia' and 'Le Roi s'amuse' (which supplied the plot for the opera of 'Rigoletto') and he insists further that one or another subdivision of this situation has been employed by Hugo at least five times in the single drama of 'Lucrèce Borgia.' If there are still any who hold that Hugo as a dramatist was "of the race and lineage of Shakspere," they may find instruction in the fact that this highly artificial situation, which the superb French lyrist was seemingly unable to leave out of his arbitrarily complicated plots, was not employed even once by the great English dramatist.

Probably nothing would have more disagreeably surprized Hugo—who held himself to be extraordinarily prolific and various, and who indeed had abundant reason for this belief—than the disclosure of the fact that he had made use so often of a single situation. And this is evidence, if any was needed, that the repetition of the same situation by the same author, or even by a succession of authors down thru the ages, is more often than not wholly unconscious, and that it is the result, not so much of any poverty of invention, as of the absolute limitation of the number of possible situations. The utmost of novelty that any plot-maker may hope to attain now in the twentieth century is only the result of his own shuffling of the same pack with which all the plot-makers of the past have been playing. A new principle he can scarcely hope to invent for himself; and all that he can safely claim for his most original sequence of scenes is a patent on the combination.

M. Polti, indeed, has bravely offered to supply ten thousand new plots, put together by combining and recombining the manifold subdivisions of his thirty-six situations, some of which he has ascertained to have been sadly neglected by the playwrights of our time. One may venture to doubt whether there would be profit in taking advantage of this generous offer, for if certain situations essayed in the past have not been popular of late, there is warrant for wondering whether this neglect is not due to an instinctive feeling on the part of the playwright of the present that these situations would fail to excite the interest of the playgoers of our own time and to evoke an emotional response. To insure the success of a play, it is not enough that the author should combine an ingenious sequence of striking scenes; he has always the spectators to reckon with also, their likes and dislikes. The practical playwright knows only too well, and often by sad experience, that the audience of to-day does not relish certain situations which run counter to its prejudices and its predilections, however pleasing these same situations may have been to audiences of the past. The duty of personal vengeance, for example—which was at the center of the tragedy-of-blood, ever delightful to Tudor theatergoers—has been disestablished by the advance of civilization; and it is therefore no longer acceptable as the dominant motive of a drama of modern life.

There is not a little significance, however, in another of M. Polti's suggestions—that perhaps a portion of the beauty and power we discern in the great plays of the Greeks was directly due to the accepted limitation of the themes which a tragic writer held himself authorized to treat. The restriction of the number of available legends forced the successive dramatists of Athens to handle again, each in his turn, the dark stories already dealt with by his predecessors. The fateful lives of Œdipus, for example, and of his family, of Agamemnon, and of his unhappy offspring—these were shown in action in the

orchestra of the theater of Dionysus again and
again, by Æschylus, by Sophocles, by Euripides,
and by many another poet-playwright of that
splendid epoch whose works have not descended
to us. Of necessity, the dramatist was nerved
to keenest endeavor by the knowledge that his
play had to withstand a comparison with other
plays presenting the same characters in the same
situations, and by the certainty that his personal
contribution would stand out sharply. A similar
ordeal was undergone by the great painters of
the Italian Renascence, who tried their hands,
almost all of them, on the Madonna with the
Holy Child, on the Descent from the Cross, and
on every other of the score of stock subjects then
in favor for the appropriate decoration of altar
and alcove and dome. There is wisdom in M.
Brunetière's assertion that "just as obedience is
the apprenticeship of command, so is imitation
the novitiate of originality."

We may be assured that this narrow limiting
of the number of themes likely to be treated by
the painters of Italy and by the playwrights of
Greece at once diminished the demand on them
for mere invention and left them free to put forth
the utmost strength of their imagination, so that
the artist could express himself fully and interpret
in his own fashion a subject certain to be handled
sooner or later by the chief of his fellow-crafts-

men. And if the descent from the sublime is not too sudden, attention might here be called to the similar method of measuring the skill of the individual performer which we perceive in a later and more scientific development of what was once almost a game of chance. In "duplicate whist," as it is called, identical hands are played in turn by a succession of players, who are thus put to the test sharply, each withstanding comparison with every one of his rivals.

A strange fascination there is in the wish that it might be possible to apply to the art of fiction —which is often little more than a game of chance —the comparative method of duplicate whist. It would be possible for us to weigh the merits of the novelists far more exactly, if we could only impose upon all of them, once in a way, the treatment of the same theme, every successive story-teller making it his own for the moment, assimilating it, handling it as he pleased, in accordance with his own instincts and his own principles. It would enable us to note how adroitly the artist in narrative could deal with a topic which he did not feel to be sympathetic or stimulating; and on the other hand, it would show us how much this author or that has been sustained by the signal good fortune which put into his hands once at least the one subject best suited to his method and his temperament. In time, it would train the critical reader in the habit of distinguishing between theme and treatment; and it would encourage him to face the task of weighing the merits of each of these separately.

Altho we cannot insist that the novelists of the twentieth century shall undergo this ordeal, we may amuse ourselves by guessing at the result if the test had been applied to the novelists of the centuries that have gone before. There is no difficulty in picking out a plot familiar to all of us now and universal in its appeal—a plot which any storyteller of any age might have chosen to develop in his own fashion. And perhaps no story is better fitted for this experiment than the heartrending tale which Shakspere took from the Italian and transfigured by his genius into the immortal tragedy of 'Romeo and Juliet.' Quarrels between rival families have been frequent enough, and young couples there have always been who loved wilfully in spite of a heritage of hate. There is a never-fading enchantment in the story of their struggles, whatever the country where they lived and died, and whatever their station in society.

How would this tale have been told in the eighteenth century by the author of 'Robinson Crusoe'? by the author of 'Clarissa Harlowe'? by the author of 'Tom Jones'? by the author of 'Tristram Shandy'? How would it have fared in the nineteenth century if Dickens had been attracted to it, or Thackeray? How would it be presented now in the twentieth century if it should be chosen again by Mr. Howells or by Mr. James? We need not ask what Mark Twain would do with it, because he has shown us in the Shepardson-Grangerford episode of 'Huckleberry Finn' that he could bring out its inherent romance, even tho he intrusted the telling to the humorous realist who was the son of the town drunkard. Nor have we to inquire how it would have presented itself to Erckmann-Chatrian, because the Alsatian collaborators made it their own in the somber pages of the 'Rantzau.'

It is not rash to assume that Defoe would have set up rival shopkeepers, one with a son and the other with a daughter; and he would have delighted in accumulating the minutest details of the daily life of the competing tradesmen. The fathers would have been sturdy Englishmen, both of them, obstinate and pious; and the preaching of a sound morality would never have been neglected. The narrative would purport to be truth; and probably it would be credited to the pen of one of the partisans, setting down in the first person a conscientious record of what he had seen with his own eyes. But if Richardson had wisht to make our ancestors weep at the wos of Romeo and the sad trials of Juliet, he would have abandoned the autobiographic form characteristic of Defoe's method of approach, for the epistolary, in which the author of 'Pamela' felt himself more at ease; and he would have spared us none of the letters of Romeo to Juliet, and of Juliet to Romeo, and of Romeo to Mercutio, and of Juliet to her nurse. The tenser the tragic gloom, the more voluminous these letters would become, the more self-analytical, and at the same time, the more pathetic. If Fielding had selected this story as the basis of a prose-epic we should have a masterly structure, perhaps distorted by an undue insistence upon Romeo's youthful intrigue with Rosaline. And if Sterne had pretended to play with this tragic tale, he would have given us the married life of Juliet's parents, with all the humorous whims of old Capulet; and after unending digressions the author might die himself before his heroine was fairly out of the arms of the nurse.

To declare how Dickens might have presented the same theme is not difficult. The tragedy would sink to tortuous melodrama, and there would be much mystery-mongering, with a careful covering up of dark secrets to be revealed only at an opportune moment. The large simplicity of the theme would be frittered away, and every opportunity for deliberate pathos would be insisted upon. Probably Juliet would die in blank verse, disguised as prose. But Mercutio, altho he would certainly cease to be a gentleman, would be a most amusing personality whose whimsical behavior would seem highly laughable; and the nurse might become another Mrs. Gamp, with a host of peculiarities realized with riotous humor. And it is possible also to make a guess at the treatment which would have been accorded to the pitiful tale if Thackeray had undertaken it. The tragedy would have softened into a tragi-comedy with a happy ending probably, the loving couple being reprieved somehow in the final chapters just before the kindly author put his puppets away, after preaching a last gentle sermon on the vanity of life. The background would be the British society of the middle of the nineteenth century; and some Lady Kew, delightfully clever and selfishly arrogant, might be the chief of one clan, and some Lord Steyne, bitter and masterful, might head the rival house. And not improbably the narrator would be Mr. Arthur Pendennis himself.

Perhaps Mr. and Mrs. March might constitute the chorus, if Mr. Howells were to lay the scene here in New York, bringing one family from the West, endowed somehow with a certain elemental largeness of mold, and importing the

other from that New England which could be
held responsible for the sensitiveness of their
self-torturing consciences. There would be no
blinking of the minor selfishnesses of humanity;
and neither hero nor heroine would stand forth
flawless. Their failures would be very human;
and the author would withhold all comment,
leaving the veracity of the portrayal to speak for
itself. There would be unrolled before the reader
the broad panorama of the cosmopolitan metropolis, infinitely variegated, often harsh in color,
but forever fascinating in the intensity of its vitality. The modern tragedy with its catastrophe
internal rather than external, would be laid before
us in a narrative containing endless miracles of
delicate observation and countless felicities of
delicate phrasing.

Like many another distinguished painter, Mr.
Henry James has at least three manners, following one another in the order of time; and there
is no certainty at which stage of his career he
might be tempted to the telling of this tale. Early
in his evolution as a novelist, he might have
seized upon it as the promising foundation for an
international complication, altho even then he
would have attenuated the more violent crudities
of the original story. Later, he might have been
lured into essaying the analysis of Juliet's senti-
ments, as she was swayed by her growing at-

tachment for Romeo, and as she was restrained by her indurated fidelity to the family tradition. More recently still, Mr. James might have perceived the possibility of puzzling us by letting us only dimly surmise what had past behind the closed doors that shut in the ill-fated lovers, and of leaving us in a maze of uncertainty and a mist of doubt, peering pitifully, and groping blindly for a clew to tangled and broken motives.

Perhaps it is idle thus to wonder how any one of a dozen novelists of distinctive talent would have treated this alluring theme had he taken it for his own.   But of this we may be certain, that any novelist of individuality who had chosen it would have made it his own, and would have sent it forth stamped with his own image and superscription.   Indeed, the same tale told by Richardson and by Sterne, altho they were contemporary sentimentalists, would have had so little in common that the careless reader might fail to see any similarity whatsoever; and probably even the pettiest of criticasters would feel no call to bring an accusation of plagiarism against either of them.

(1905.)

INVENTION AND IMAGINATION

INVENTION AND IMAGINATION

PROBABLY not a few readers of Prof. Barrett Wendell's suggestive lectures on the 'Temper of the Seventeenth Century in English Literature' were surprized to be told that a chief peculiarity of the greatest of dramatic poets "was a somewhat sluggish avoidance of needless invention. When anyone else had done a popular thing, Shakspere was pretty sure to imitate him and to do it better. But he hardly ever did anything first." In other words, Shakspere was seeking, above all else, to please the contemporary playgoers; and he was prompt to undertake any special type of piece they had shown a liking for; so we can see him borrowing, one after another, the outer form of the chronicle-play from Marlowe, of the tragedy-of-blood from Kyd, of romantic-comedy from Greene, and of dramatic-romance from Beaumont and Fletcher. And in like manner Molière was content to return again and again to the type of play which he had taken over from the Italian comedy-of-masks.

This "sluggish avoidance of needless invention," which is characteristic of Shakspere—and of Molière also, altho in a less degree—is evidenced not only by their eager adoption of an accepted type of play, an outer form of approved popularity, it is obvious also in their plots, wherein we find situations, episodes, incidents drawn from all sorts of sources. In all the two-score of Shakspere's plays, comic and tragic and historic, there are very few, indeed, the stories of which are wholly of his own making. The invention of Molière is not quite so sluggish; and there are probably three or four of his plays the plots of which seem to be more or less his own; but even in building up these scant exceptions he never hesitated to levy on the material available in the two hundred volumes of uncatalogued French and Spanish and Italian plays, set down in the inventory of his goods drawn up at his death. Apparently Shakspere and Molière accepted in advance Goethe's theory that much time may be lost in mere invention, whereas, "with a given material all goes easier and better. Facts and characters being provided, the poet has only the task of animating the whole. He preserves his own fulness . . . since he has only the trouble of execution."

It has long been a commonplace of criticism that great poets seldom invent their myths; and it may in time become a commonplace of criti-

cism that they seldom invent their forms. But
in default of the lesser invention, they have the
larger imagination; and there is no pedantry in
seeking to emphasize the distinction between
these two qualities, often carelessly confused.
Invention is external and imagination is internal.
The poets, by the mere fact that they are poets,
possess the power of imagination, which alone
gives vitality and significance to the ready-made
plots they are willing to run into ready-made
molds. Invention can do no more than devise;
imagination can interpret. The details of ' Romeo and Juliet ' may be more or less contained
in the tale of the Italian novelist; but the inner
meaning of that ideal tragedy of youthful love is
seized and set forth only by the English dramatist.

Imagination in its fullest meaning must be held
to include invention; but invention is only one
of the less important elements of imagination;
and it is the element which seems to be more or
less negligible when the other elements are amply
developed. La Fontaine, one of the most individual of French poets, devised only a few—and
not the best—of the delightful fables he related
with unfailing felicity. Calderon, who was the
most imaginative of the dramatists of Spain, was
perhaps the least inventive of them all, content-
edly availing himself of the situations, and even
of the complete plots of his more fertile fellow-

playwrights; and two of his most characteristic dramas, for example, two in which he has most adequately exprest himself, the 'Alcalde of Zalamea' and the 'Physician of His Own Honor,' are borrowed almost bodily from his fecund contemporary Lope de Vega. Racine seems to have found a special pleasure in treating anew the themes Euripides had already dealt with almost a score of centuries earlier. Tennyson, to take another example, displayed not a little of this "sluggish avoidance of needless invention," often preferring to apply his imagination to the transfiguring of what Malory or Miss Mitford, Froude or Freeman had made ready for his hand. This eschewing of overt originality fitted him all the more to be spokesman of his time, and to voice the ideals of his race and of his day. Tennyson, so Sir Leslie Stephen told us, " could express what occurred to everybody in language that could be approached by nobody." Browning, on the other hand, made his own plots, and on the whole made them none too well, especially in his dramatic poems, in the structure of which he was entirely neglectful of the accepted forms of the theater of his own time—accepted forms of which Shakspere and Molière would have availed themselves instinctively. It was not Browning, but Whitman—and Whitman in 1855, when the bard of Manhattan had not yet shown the stuff that was in him—that Lowell had in mind in the letter where he says " when a man aims at originality he acknowledges himself consciously unoriginal. . . . The great fellows have always let the stream of their activity flow quietly."

What is true of the poets is true also of the painters; and Lowell, who did not lose his Yankee shrewdness in the galleries of Italy, saw this also and phrased it happily in another of his letters. " The great merit, it seems to me, of the old painters was that they did not try to be original." The old painters were following in the footsteps of painters still older, from whom they received the accepted formulas for representing the subjects most likely to be ordered by customers. These accepted formulas representing the Annunciation, for instance, the Disputing in the Temple, the Crucifixion even, were passed down from one generation of artists to another; and in each successive generation the greatest painter was generally he who had no strong desire to be different from his fellows, and who was quite willing to express himself in the patterns which were then accepted traditions of his craft. To a student of the work of the generation that went before, there is often little or no invention in some of the mightiest masterpieces of painting, however much imagination there may be. The painters who wrought these masterpieces were only doing what their immediate predecessors had been doing, the same thing more or less in the same way—but with infinitely more insight, power, and inspiration. As Professor Butcher has put it tersely, " the creative art of genius does not consist in bringing something out of nothing, but in taking possession of material that exists, in appropriating it, interpreting it anew."

In the very ingenious and highly original tale called the ' Murders in the Rue Morgue,' the earliest of all detective-stories, Poe displayed his remarkable gift of invention; but he revealed his share of penetrative imagination far more richly in the simpler story of the ' Fall of the House of Usher.' Wilkie Collins had more invention than Dickens, as Dickens had more than Thackeray. Indeed, Thackeray, indolent as he was by temperament, was not infrequently " sluggish in his avoidance of needless invention." He kept his eye intent on the lurking inconsistencies of human nature, and did not give his best thought to the more mechanical element of the novelist's art. Cooper and Dumas were far more fertile in the invention of situations than was Thackeray; and even Scott, careless as he was in his easy habit of narration, gave more of his thought to the constructing of unexpected scenes.

Three centuries ago Sidney asserted that "it is not riming and versing that maketh a poet, no

more than a long gown maketh an advocate";
and to-day we know that it is not skill in plot-
making or ingenuity in devising unforeseen situations which proves the story-teller's possession
of imagination. It is scarcely needful now to
repeat that 'Called Back' and 'She'—good
enough stories, both of them, each in its kind—
did not demand a larger imaginative effort on the
part of their several authors than was required to
write the 'Rise of Silas Lapham' or 'Daisy Mil-
ler.' More invention there may be in the late
Hugh Conway's tale and in Mr. Haggard's startling narrative of the phenix-female; but it is invention that we discover in their strange stories
rather than imagination. Indeed, he is an ill-
equipt critic who does not recognize the fact that
it calls for less imagination to put together a sequence of unexpected happenings such as we
enjoy in the fictions of the neo-romanticists than
is needed to vitalize and make significant the less
exciting portrayals of character which we find in
the finer narratives of the true realists.

It was Dr. Johnson who declared, rather ponderously, it is true, but none the less shrewdly,
that "the irregular combinations of fanciful invention may delight a while by that novelty of
which the common satiety of life sends us all in
quest; but the pleasures of sudden wonder are
soon exhausted and the many can only repose on

the stability of truth." Johnson was speaking here from the point of view of the reader only; but he might have noted also that the " irregular combinations of fanciful invention " tend to lose their interest even for the very writers who have been successful in supplying their readers with the "pleasures of sudden wonder." For example, in the opening years of this twentieth century the witty historian of the kingdom of Zenda—that land of irresponsible adventure which lies seemingly between the Forest of Arden and the unexplored empire of Weissnichtwo—this historian, after regaling us with brisk and brilliant chronicles of that strange country and of the adjacent territory, apparently wearied of these pleasant inventions of his and wisht to come to a closer grapple with the realities of life and character. But he soon found that this task was not so easy as it appeared—not so easy, indeed, as the earlier writing had been; and ' Quisanté,' for all its cleverness, did not prove its author's possession of the informing imagination which alone can give life and meaning to a novel dealing with men and women as they are in the real world.

Not unlike is the case of the narrator of the manifold and varied deductions of Mr. Sherlock Holmes, that British reincarnation of Poe's M. Dupin. There is danger of unfairness in accept-

ing the authenticity of words put into a man's
mouth by any interviewer, however well inten-
tioned; and there is, therefore, a possibility that
the biographer of the Brigadier Gerard did not
confess his own slight esteem for the many tales
of invented adventure which had given him his
wide-spread popularity. But there is an accent
of veracity in the reported assertion of the author
of 'A Duet with an Occasional Chorus' that this
is the book closest to his heart, because it is an
honest attempt to deal with the facts of life as
they stare us in the face to-day. And yet 'A
Duet' is unknown to a tithe of the countless
readers who have devoured its writer's other volumes with avidity. And what is more to the
point, it does not—favorite of its author tho it
is—it does not deserve to be known so widely.
This is because it is not so good as the other
books of the same writer, not so good in its
kind as they are in theirs. The tales that dealt
with Sherlock Holmes and Brigadier Gerard and
the White Company are works of invention
mainly; and the writer had proved himself capable of adroit and ingenious invention. 'A Duet,'
dealing with the commonplaces of life, needed
not invention, which would indeed almost be out
of place in a humdrum chronicle; it demanded
imagination to interpret the commonplace and to
transfigure the humdrum, revealing their essen-

tial significance. And this imagination the author had not at his call, in spite of his command over the more showy invention.

It may not be without interest to consider how another writer of our time, not seeking for originality, happened to find it, and how his acceptance of certain literary patterns, so to call them—patterns inherited from the remote and shadowy past of our race—led him to an unforeseen effort of illuminative imagination, which suddenly elevated what he had done and gave it a significance far wider and far deeper than the author had foreseen. In the two successive volumes of the 'Jungle Book' (as it was originally published) there are two sets of stories commingled and yet sharply distinct. One group deals with the boyhood of Mowgli among the beasts of the forest; and to many of us these linked tales represent the highest achievement of Mr. Kipling's genius; they seem as assured of survival as anything which the nineteenth century has transmitted to the twentieth. The other stories, the 'White Seal' and the 'Undertakers' and their companions, stand on a lower level; they are good stories, no doubt,—very good, indeed, one or two of them. But they have an added importance in that they seem to have been the needful accompaniment of the Mowgli tales; they may be considered as the underbrush that at first protected the growth of the loftier tree.

They are modern examples of the beast-fable, latter-day amplifications of the simple tale of animals credited with human cunning, such as primitive man told to his naked children as they huddled around the embers in the cave, which was then their only home. The beast-fable is a literary pattern of an undiscoverable antiquity, as alluring to-day as ever before, since the child in us fortunately never dies. It is a pattern which Mr. Kipling has handled with a constant affection and with a large freedom. His earlier animal tales dealt with wild beasts, or at least with the creatures of the forests and of the ocean beyond the influence of man and remote from his haunts. Soon he availed himself of the same pattern to tell stories of animals domesticated and in close contact with man; and thus he gave us the 'Walking Delegate' and the 'Maltese Cat.' In time he took a further step and applied to the iron horse of the railroad the method which had enabled him to set before us the talk of the polo pony and of the blooded trotter; and thus he was led to compose '007,' in which we see the pattern of the primitive beast-fable so stretched as to enable us to overhear the intimate conversation of humanized locomotives, the steeds of steel that puff and pant in and out of the roundhouse in an American railroad yard. Yet one more extension of the pattern enabled him to take a final step; after having given a human soul to separate engines, he proceeded then to animate the several parts of a single machine. And thus we have 'How the Ship Found Herself' and the later 'Below the Mill-dam.' But altho these are successive stages of the primitive beast-fable as it has been modified in Mr. Kipling's restless hands, there is little flagrant originality, even at the end, since 'How the Ship Found Herself' is seen to be only an up-to-date version of one of the earliest fables, the 'Belly and the Members.'

Interesting as it may be to clamber up into the spreading family-tree of fiction, it is not here that we must seek for the stem from which the Mowgli stories ultimately flowered. These stories are not directly derived from the beast-fable, altho his mastery of that literary pattern may have helped the author to find his final form. They are a development from one of his own tales, 'In the Rukh,' included at first in 'Many Inventions,' and now transferred to itc proper place at the end of the book in which the adventures of Mowgli are recorded. In that first tale, which is now the last, we have set before us the impression Mowgli and his little brothers, the wolves, made upon two white men in the Indian service; and incidentally we are permitted to snatch a glimpse or two of Mowgli's youth in the jungle. But the story is told from the point of view of these white men; and it is small wonder that when the author came to look again at what he had written he saw how rich it was in its possibilities. He was moved to go back to narrate the whole series of Mowgli's adventures from the very beginning, with Mowgli himself as the center of the narrative and with little obtrusion of the white man's civilization.

There was invention in this early story, and imagination also, altho not so abundant. But as the author brooded over the incidents of Mowgli's babyhood there in the thick of the forest, in the midst of the beasts, whose blood-brother he became, suddenly his imagination revealed to him that the jungle and all its inhabitants must be governed by law, or else it was a realm of chaos. It is this portrayal of wild life subject to an immitigable code which gives its sustaining moral to the narrative of Mowgli's career. As Mr. Kipling said to me once, "When I had found the Law of the Jungle the rest was easy!" For him it may have been easy, since his invention is ever fresh and fertile; but the finding of the Law of the Jungle—that transcended mere invention with all its multiplied ingenuities—that was a stroke of imagination.

This distinction between imagination and invention may not be as important as that between imagination and fancy urged by Wordsworth a century ago; and no doubt there is always dan-

ger in any undue insistence upon catchwords,
which are often empty of meaning, and which
are sometimes employed to convey a misleading
suggestion. This distinction has its own importance, however, and it is not empty or misleading. It needs to be accepted in art as it has
been accepted in science, in which domain a
fertile discovery is recognized as possible only to
the imagination, while a specific device is
spoken of as an invention. Newton and Darwin
were discoverers by their possession of imagination; whereas the telegraph and the telephone
are to be credited to humbler inventors, making
application of principles already discovered.

This opening century of ours is an era of extraordinary dexterity and of wide-spread cleverness, and we need to be put on our guard against
the risk of mistaking the products of our abundant invention for the rarer gifts of inspiring
imagination. It is well for us to be reminded
now and again that the great masters, painters
and poets alike, novelists and dramatists, have
often displayed "a sluggish avoidance of needless invention" at the very minute when their
robust imagination was putting forth its full
strength.

(1904.)

POE AND THE DETECTIVE-STORY

POE AND THE DETECTIVE-STORY

I

IN one of those essays which were often as
speculative and suggestive as he claimed, the
late John Addington Symonds called attention to
three successive phases of criticism, pointing out
that the critics had first set up as judges, delivering opinions from the bench and never hesitating
to put on the black cap; that then they had
changed into showmen, dwelling chiefly on the
beauties of the masterpieces they were exhibiting;
and that finally, and only very recently, they had
become natural historians, studying "each object
in relation to its antecedents and its consequences" and making themselves acquainted
"with the conditions under which the artist
grew, the habits of his race, the opinions of his
age, his physiological and psychological peculiarities." And Symonds might have added that
it is only in this latest phase, when the critics
have availed themselves of the methods of the
comparative biologists, that they are concerned

with the interesting problems connected with the
origin of the several literary species.

All over the world to-day devoted students are
working at the hidden history of the lyric, for
example, and of certain subdivisions of this species, such as the elegy, as it flowered long ago in
Greece and as it has flourished in most of the literatures of modern Europe. To the "natural historian" of literary art, these subdivisions of a species are becoming more and more interesting, as
he perceives more clearly how prone the poets
have always been to work in accord with the
pattern popular in their own time and to express
themselves freely in the form they found ready to
their hands. The student of the English drama
is delighted when he can seize firmly the rise and
fall of the tragedy-of-blood for one example, of
the comedy-of-humors for another, and of senti-
mental-comedy for a third; just as the investi-
gator into the annals of fiction is pleased to be
able to trace the transformations of the pastoral,
of the picaresque romance, and of the later short-
story.

The beginnings of a species, or of a subspecies,
are obscure more often than not; and they are
rarely to be declared with certainty. "Nothing
is more difficult than to discover who have been
in literature the first inventors" of a new form,
so M. Jules Lemaître once asserted, adding that

innovations have generally been attempted by writers of no great value, and not infrequently by those who failed in those first efforts, unable to profit by their own originality. And it is natural enough that a good many sighting shots should be wasted on a new target before even an accomplished marksman could plump his bullet in the bull's-eye. The historical novel as we know it now must be credited to Scott, who preluded by the rather feeble 'Waverley,' before attaining the more boldly planned 'Rob Roy' and 'Guy Mannering.' The sea-tale is to be ascribed to Cooper, whose wavering faith in its successful accomplishment is reflected in the shifting of the successive episodes of the 'Pilot' from land to water and back again to land; and it was only when he came to write the 'Red Rover' that Cooper displayed full confidence in the form he had been the first to experiment with. But the history of the detective-story begins with the publication of the 'Murders in the Rue Morgue a masterpiece of its kind, which even its author was unable to surpass; and Poe, unlike most other originators, rang the bell the very first time he took aim.

II

THE detective - story which Poe invented sharply differentiates itself from the earlier tales of mystery, and also from the later narratives in which actual detectives figure incidentally. Perhaps the first of these tales of mystery is Walpole's 'Castle of Otranto,' which appears to us now clumsy enough, with its puerile attempts to excite terror. The romances of Mrs. Radcliffe are scarcely more solidly built—indeed, the fatigue of the sophisticated reader of to-day when he undertakes the perusal of these old-fashioned and long-winded chronicles may be ascribed partly to the flimsiness of the foundation which is supposed to support the awe-inspiring superstructure. Godwin's 'Caleb Williams' is far more firmly put together; and its artful planning called for imagination as well as mere invention. In the 'Edgar Huntley' of Charles Brockden Brown the veil of doubt skilfully shrouds the unsuspected and the unsuspecting murderer who did the evil deed in his sleep—anticipating the somnambulist hero of Wilkie Collins's 'Moonstone.'

The disadvantages of this mystery-mongering have been pointed out by Poe with his wonted acuteness in his criticism of ' Barnaby Rudge.' After retelling the plot of Dickens's contorted narrative, and after putting the successive episodes into their true sequence, Poe asserted that "the thesis of the novel may thus be regarded as based upon curiosity," and he declared that "every point is so arranged as to perplex the reader and whet his desire for elucidation." He insisted "that the secret be well kept is obviously necessary," because if it leaks out "against the author's will, his purposes are immediately at odds and ends." Then he remarked that altho "there can be no question that . . . many points . . . which would have been comparatively insipid even if given in full detail in a natural sequence, are endued with the interest of mystery; but neither can it be denied that a vast many more points are at the same time deprived of all effect, and become null, through the impossibility of comprehending them without the key." In other words, the novelist has chosen to sacrifice to the fleeting interest which is evoked only by wonder the more abiding interest which is aroused by the clear perception of the inter-play of character and motive. Poe suggested that even 'Barnaby Rudge'—in spite of its author's efforts to keep secret the real springs of action which controlled the characters—if taken up a second time by a reader put into possession of all that had been concealed, would be found to possess quadruple brilliance, "a brilliance unprofitably sacrificed at the shrine of the keenest interest of mere mystery."

Dickens was not the last novelist of note to be

tempted and to fall into this snare. In the 'Disciple,' and again in 'André Cornélis' M. Paul Bourget was lured from the path of psychologic analysis into the maze of mystery-mongering; but he had the tact to employ his secrets to excite interest only in the beginning of what were, after all, studies from life, each of them setting forth the struggle of a man with the memory of his crime. In the 'Wreckers' Stevenson and his young collaborator attempted that "form of police novel or mystery-story which consisted in beginning your yarn anywhere but at the beginning, and finishing it anywhere but at the end." They were attracted by its "peculiar interest when done, and the peculiar difficulties that attend its execution." They were "repelled by that appearance of insincerity and shallowness of tone which seems its inevitable drawback," because "the mind of the reader always bent to pick up clews receives no impression of reality or life, rather of an airless, elaborate mechanism; and the book remains enthralling, but insignificant, like a game of chess, not a work of human art." They hoped to find a new way of handling the old tale of mystery, so that they might get the profit without paying the price. But already in his criticism of 'Barnaby Rudge' had Poe showed why disappointment was unavoidable, because the more artfully the dark intimations of horror are held out, the more certain it is that the anticipation must surpass the reality. No matter how terrific the circumstances may be which shall appear to have occasioned the mystery, "still they will not be able to satisfy the mind of the reader. He will surely be disappointed."

Even Balzac, with all his mastery of the novelist's art, lost more than he gained when he strove to arouse the interest of his readers by an appeal to their curiosity. His mystery-mongering is sometimes perilously close to blatant sensationalism and overt charlatanry; and he seems to be seeking the bald effect for its own sake. In the 'Chouans,' and again in the 'Ténébreuse Affaire,' he has complicated plots and counterplots entangled almost to confusion, but the reader "receives no impression of reality or life" even if these novels cannot be dismist as empty examples of "airless, elaborate mechanism."

The members of the secret police appearing in these stories have all a vague likeness to Vidocq, whose alleged memoirs were published in 1828, a few years before the author of the 'Human Comedy' began to deal with the scheming of the underworld. Balzac's spies and his detectives are not convincing, despite his utmost effort; and we do not believe in their preternatural acuteness. Even in the conduct of their intrigues we are lost in a murky mistiness. Balzac is at his best when he is arousing the emotions of recognition; and he is at his worst when he sinks to evoking the emotions of surprise.

III

In the true detective-story as Poe conceived it in the 'Murders of the Rue Morgue,' it is not in the mystery itself that the author seeks to interest the reader, but rather in the successive steps whereby his analytic observer is enabled to solve a problem that might well be dismist as beyond human elucidation. Attention is centered on the unraveling of the tangled skein rather than on the knot itself. The emotion aroused is not mere surprize, it is recognition of the unsuspected capabilities of the human brain; it is not a wondering curiosity as to an airless mechanism, but a heightening admiration for the analytic acumen capable of working out an acceptable answer to the puzzle propounded. In other words, Poe, while he availed himself of the obvious advantages of keeping a secret from his readers and of leaving them guessing as long as he pleased, shifted the point of attack and succeeded in giving a human interest to his tale of wonder.

And by this shift Poe transported the detective-story from the group of tales of adventure into the group of portrayals of character. By bestowing upon it a human interest, he raised it in the literary scale. There is no need now to exaggerate the merits of this feat or to suggest that Poe himself was not capable of loftier efforts. Of course the ' Fall of the House of Usher,' which is of imagination all compact, is more valid evidence of his genius than the ' Murders in the Rue Morgue,' which is the product rather of his invention, supremely ingenious as it is. Even tho the detective-story as Poe produced it is elevated far above the barren tale of mystery which preceded it and which has been revived in our own day, it is not one of the loftiest of literary forms, and its possibilities are severely limited. It suffers today from the fact that in the half century and more since Poe set the pattern it has been vulgarized, debased, degraded by a swarm of imitators who lacked his certainty of touch, his instinctive tact, his intellectual individuality. In their hands it has been bereft of its distinction and despoiled of its atmosphere.

Even at its best, in the simple perfection of form that Poe bestowed on it, there is no denying that it demanded from its creator no depth of sentiment, no warmth of emotion, and no large understanding of human desire. There are those who would dismiss it carelessly, as making an

appeal not far removed from that of the riddle and
of the conundrum.   There are those again who
would liken it rather to the adroit trick of a
clever conjurer.   No doubt, it gratifies in us
chiefly that delight in difficulty conquered, which
is a part of the primitive play-impulse potent in
us all, but tending to die out as we grow older,
as we lessen in energy, and as we feel more
deeply the tragi-comedy of existence.   But inexpensive as it may seem to those of us who look
to literature for enlightenment, for solace in the
hour of need, for stimulus to stiffen the will in
the never-ending struggle of life, the detective
tale, as Poe contrived it, has merits of its own
as distinct and as undeniable, as those of the historical novel, for example, or of the sea-tale.   It
may please the young rather than the old, but
the pleasure it can give is ever innocent; and the
young are always in the majority.

IV

In so far as Poe had any predecessor in the
composing of a narrative, the interest of which
should reside in the application of human intelligence to the solution of a mystery, this was
not Balzac,—altho the American romancer was
sufficiently familiar with the 'Human Comedy'

122

to venture quotation from it. Nor was this predecessor Cooper, whom Balzac admired and even
imitated, altho Leatherstocking in tracking his
redskin enemies revealed the tense observation
and the faculty of deduction with which Poe
was to endow his Dupin. The only predecessor
with a good claim to be considered a progenitor
is Voltaire, in whose 'Zadig' we can find the
method which Poe was to apply more elaborately.
The Goncourts perceived this descent of Poe from
Voltaire when they recorded in their 'Journal'
that the strange tales of the American poet
seemed to them to belong to "a new literature,
the literature of the twentieth century, scientifi-
cally miraculous story-telling by A + B, a literature at once monomaniac and mathematical,
Zadig as district-attorney, Cyrano de Bergerac as
a pupil of Arago."

Voltaire tells us that Zadig by study gained "a
sagacity which discovered to him a thousand
differences where other men saw only uniformity"; and he describes a misadventure which
befell Zadig when he was living in the kingdom
of Babylon. One day the chief eunuch asked if
he had seen the queen's dog. "It 's a female,
is n't it?" returned Zadig; "a spaniel, and very
small; she littered not long ago; she is lame of
the left forefoot; and she has very long ears."
"So you have seen her?" cried the eunuch.

"No," Zadig answered; "I have never seen her; and I never even knew that the queen had a dog."

About the same time the handsomest horse in the king's stables escaped; and the chief huntsman, meeting Zadig, inquired if he had not seen the animal. And Zadig responded: "It is the horse that gallops the best; he is five feet high; his shoe is very small; his tail is three and a half feet long; the knobs of his bit are of twenty-three-carat gold; and he is shod with eleven-penny silver." And the chief huntsman asked, "Which way did he go?" To which Zadig replied: "I have not seen him; and I have never heard anything about him."

The chief eunuch and the chief huntsman naturally believed that Zadig had stolen the queen's dog and the king's horse; so they had him arrested and condemned, first to the knout, and afterward to exile for life in Siberia. And then both the missing animals were recovered; so Zadig was allowed to plead his case. He swore that he had never seen either the dog of the queen or the horse of the king. This is what had happened: He had been walking toward a little wood and he had seen on the sand the track of an animal, and he judged that it had been a dog. Little furrows scratched in the low hillocks of sand between the footprints showed him that it was a female whose teats were pendent, and who therefore must have littered recently. As the sand was less deeply marked by one foot than by the three others, he had perceived the queen's dog to be lame.

As for the larger quadruped, Zadig, while walking in a narrow path in the wood, had seen the prints of a horse's shoes, all at an equal distance; and he had said to himself that here was a steed with a perfect stride. The path was narrow, being only seven feet wide, and here and there the dust had been flicked from the trees on either hand, and so Zadig had made sure that the horse had a tail three and a half feet long. The branches crossed over the path at the height of five feet, and as leaves had been broken off, the observer had decided that the horse was just five feet high. As to the bit, this must be of gold, since the horse had rubbed it against a stone, which Zadig had recognized as a touchstone and on which he had assayed the trace of precious metal. And from the marks left by the horse's shoes on another kind of stone Zadig had felt certain that they were made of eleven-penny silver.

Huxley has pointed out that the method of Zadig is the method which has made possible the incessant scientific discovery of the last century. It is the method of Wellington at Assaye, assuming that there must be a ford at a certain place on the river, because there was a village on each side. It is the method of Grant at Vicksburg, examining the knapsacks of the Confederate soldiers slain in a sortie to see if these contained rations, which would show that the garrison was seeking to break out because the place was untenable. It is also the method of Poe in the 'Gold-Bug' and in the 'Murders of the Rue Morgue.' In all probability Poe borrowed it directly from Voltaire, who had taken it over from Oriental folklore.

In his application of this method, not casually, playfully, and with satiric intent, as Voltaire had applied it, but seriously and taking it as the mainspring of his story, Poe added an ingenious improvement of his own devising. Upon the preternaturally acute observer who was to control the machinery of the tale, the American poet bestowed a companion of only an average alertness and keenness; and to this commonplace companion the romancer confided the telling of the story. By this seemingly simple device Poe doubled the effectiveness of his work, because this unobservant and unimaginative narrator of the unraveling of a tangled skein by an observant and imaginative analyst naturally recorded his own admiration and astonishment as the wonder was wrought before his eyes, so that the admiration and astonishment were transmitted directly and suggestively, to the readers of the narrative.

In the 'Gold-Bug' the wonder-worker is Legrand, and in both the 'Murders in the Rue Morgue' and the 'Purloined Letter' he is M. Dupin; and in all three tales the telling of the story is entrusted to an anonymous narrator, serving not only as a sort of Greek chorus to hint to the spectators the emotions they ought to feel, but also as the describer of the personality and peculiarities of Legrand and Dupin, who are thus individualized, humanized, and related to the real world. If they had not been accepted by the narrator as actual beings of flesh and blood, they might otherwise retain the thinness and the dryness of disembodied intelligences working in a vacuum.

This device of the transmitting narrator is indisputably valuable; and, properly enough, it reappears in the one series of detective tales which may be thought by some to rival Poe's. The alluring record of the investigations of Mr. Sherlock Holmes is the work of a certain Dr. Watson, a human being but little more clearly characterized than the anonymous narrators who have preserved for us the memory of Legrand and Dupin. But Poe here again exhibited a more artistic reserve than any of his imitators, in so far as he refrained from the undue laudation of the strange intellectual feats which are the central interest of these three tales. In the 'Gold-Bug' he even heightens his suspense by allowing the narrator to suggest that Legrand might be of unsound mind; and in the 'Murders in the Rue Morgue the narrator, altho lost in astonishment at the acuteness of Dupin, never permits his admiration to become fulsome; he holds himself in, as tho fearing that overpraise might provoke a denial. Moreover, Poe refrained from all exhibitions of Dupin's skill merely for its own sake—exhibitions only dazzling the spectators and not furthering his immediate purpose.

Nothing could be franker than Sir Conan Doyle's acknowledgment of his indebtedness. "Edgar Allen Poe, who, in his carelessly prodigal fashion, threw out the seeds from which so many of our present forms of literature have sprung, was the father of the detective tale, and covered its limits so completely that I fail to see how his followers can find any fresh ground which they can confidently call their own. For the secret of the thinness and also of the intensity of the detective-story is that the writer is left with only one quality, that of intellectual acuteness, with which to endow his hero. Everything else is outside the picture and weakens the effect. The problem and its solution must form the theme, and the character drawing is limited and subordinate. On this narrow path the writer must walk, and he sees the footmarks of Poe always in front of him. He is happy if he ever finds the means of breaking away and striking out on some little side-track of his own."

The deviser of the adventures of Sherlock Holmes hit on a happy phrase when he declared that "the problem and its solution must form the theme." This principle was violated by Dumas, in the 'Vicomte de Bragelonne,' giving us the solution before the problem, when he showed how d'Artagnan used the method of Zadig to deduce all the details of the duel on horseback, after the author had himself described to us the incidents of that fight. But when he was thus discounting his effect Dumas probably had in mind, not Poe, but Cooper, whose observant redskins he mightily admired and whom he frankly imitated in the 'Mohicans of Paris.'

V

ALTHO Poe tells these three stories in the first person, as if he was himself only the recorder of the marvelous deeds of another, both Legrand and Dupin are projections of his own personality; they are characters created by him to be endowed with certain of his own qualifications and peculiarities. They were called into being to be possest of the inventive and analytical powers of Poe himself. "To be an artist, first and always, requires a turn for induction and analysis" —so Mr. Stedman has aptly put it; and this turn for induction and analysis Poe had far more obviously than most artists. When he was a student he excelled in mathematics; in all his other tales he displays the same power of logical construction; and he delighted in the exercise of his own acumen, vaunting his ability to translate any cipher that might be sent to him and succeeding in making good his boast. In the criticism of 'Barnaby Rudge,' and again in the explanation of the Maelzel chess-player, Poe used for himself the same faculty of divination, the same power of seizing the one clue needful, however tangled amid other threads, which he had bestowed upon Legrand and Dupin.

If we may exclude the 'Marie Roget' narrative in which Poe was working over an actual case of murder, we find him only three times undertaking the "tale of ratiocination," to use his own term; and in all three stories he was singularly happy in the problem he invented for solution. For each of the three he found a fit theme, wholly different from that employed in either of the others. He adroitly adjusted the proper accessories, and he created an appropriate atmosphere. With no sense of strain, and no awkwardness of manner, he dealt with episodes strange indeed, but so simply treated as to seem natural, at least for the moment. There is no violence of intrigue or conjecture; indeed Poe strives to suggest a background of the commonplace against which his marvels may seem the more marvelous. In none of his stories is Poe's consummate mastery of the narrative art, his ultimate craftsmanship, his certain control of all the devices of the most accomplished story-teller, more evident than in these three.

And yet they are but detective-stories, after all; and Poe himself, never prone to underestimate what he had written, spoke of them lightly and even hinted that they had been overpraised. Probably they were easy writing—for him—and therefore they were not so close to his heart as certain other of his tales over which he had toiled long and laboriously. Probably also he felt the detective-story to be an inferior form. However superior his stories in this kind might be, he knew them to be unworthy of comparison with his more imaginative tales, which he had filled with a thrilling weirdness and which attained a soaring elevation far above any height to be achieved by ingenious narratives setting forth the solving of a puzzle.

It is in a letter to Philip Pendleton Cooke, written in 1846, that Poe disparaged his detective-stories and declared that they "owe most of their popularity to being something in a new key. I do not mean to say that they are not ingenious—but people think them more ingenious than they are—on account of their method and *air* of method. In the 'Murders in the Rue Morgue,' for instance, where is the ingenuity of unraveling a web which you yourself (the author) have woven for the express purpose of unraveling? The reader is made to confound the ingenuity of the supposititious Dupin with that of the writer of the story." Here, surely, Poe is over-modest; at least he over-states the case against himself. The ingenuity of the author obviously lies in his invention of a web which seemingly cannot be unraveled and which nevertheless one of the characters of the tale, Legrand or Dupin, succeeds in unraveling at last. This ingenuity may be, in one way, less than that required to solve an actual problem in real life; but it is also, in another way, more, for it had to invent its own puzzle and to put this together so that the secret seemed to be absolutely hidden, altho all the facts needed to solve it were plainly presented to the reader.

In the same letter to Cooke, Poe remarked on the " wide diversity and variety " of his tales when contrasted one with another; and he asserted that he did not consider any one better than another. "There is a vast variety of kinds, and in degree of value these kinds vary—but each tale is equally good *of its kind*." He added that "the loftiest kind is that of the highest imagination." For this reason only he considered that 'Ligeia' might be called the best of his stories. Now, after a lapse of threescore years, the 'Fall of the House of Usher,' with its "serene and somber beauty," would seem to deserve the first place of all. And among the detective-stories, standing on a lower plane as they do, because they were wrought by invention rather than by the interpreting imagination, the foremost position may be given to the 'Murders in the Rue Morgue.' In this tale Poe's invention is most ingenious and his subject is selected with the fullest understanding of the utmost possibilities of the detective-story. At the core of it is a strange, mysterious, monstrous crime; and M. Anatole France was never wiser than when he declared the unfailing interest of mankind in a gigantic misdeed "because we find in all crimes that fund of hunger and desire on which we all live, the good as well as the bad." Before a crime such as this we seem to find ourselves peering into the contorted visage of primitive man, obeying no law but his own caprice.

The superiority of the poet who wrote the first detective-story over all those who have striven to tread in the trail he blazed is obvious enough. It resides not only in his finer workmanship, his more delicate art, his surer certainty of execution, his more absolute knowledge of what it was best to do and of the way best to do this; it is to be seen not only in his command of verisimilitude, in his plausibility, in his faculty of enwrapping the figures of his narrative in the atmosphere most fit for them; it is not in any of these things or in all of them that Poe's supremacy is founded. The reason of that supremacy must be sought in the fact that, after all, Poe was a poet, and that he had the informing imagination of a poet, even tho it was only the more prosaic side of the faculty divine which he chose to employ in these tales of ratiocination.

It is by their possession of poetry, however slight their portion might be, that Fitzjames O'Brien and M. Jean Richepin and Mr. Rudyard Kipling were kept from frank failure when they followed in Poe's footsteps and sought to imitate, or at least to emulate his more largely imaginative tales in the 'Diamond Lens' of the Irish-American, in the 'Morts Bizarres' of the Frenchman, and in half a dozen tales of the Anglo-Indian. But what tincture of poesy, what sweep of vision, what magic of style, is there in the attempts of the most of the others who have taken pattern by Poe's detective-stories? None, and less than none. Ingenuity of a kind there is in Gaboriau's longer fictions, and in those of Fortuné du Bois-gobey, and in those of Wilkie Collins; but this ingenuity is never so simply employed, and it is often artificial and violent and mechanical. It exists for its own sake, with little relation to the admitted characteristics of our common human-ity. It stands alone, and it is never accompanied by the apparent ease which adds charm to Poe's handling of his puzzles.

Consider how often Gaboriau puts us off with a broken-backed narrative, taking up his curtain on a promising problem, presenting it to us in aspects of increasing difficulty, only at last to confess his impotence by starting afresh and slowly detailing the explanatory episodes which happened before the curtain rose. Consider how frequently Fortuné du Boisgobey failed to play fair. Consider how juiceless was the documen-tary method of Wilkie Collins, how mechanical and how arid, how futilely complicated, how prolonged, and how fatiguing. Consider all the minor members of the sorry brood hatched out of the same egg, how cheap and how childish the most of them are. Consider all these; and we are forced to the conclusion that if the writ-ing of a good detective-story is so rare and so difficult, if only one of Poe's imitators has been able really to rival his achievement, if this single

success has been the result of an acceptance of
Poe's formula and of a close adherence to Poe's
practise, then, what Poe wrought is really unique;
and we must give him the guerdon of praise
due to an artist who has accomplished the first
time of trying that which others have failed to
achieve even after he had shown them how.

(1904.)

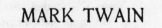

MARK TWAIN

[This biographical criticism was written to serve as an introduction to the complete edition of Mark Twain's Works.]

MARK TWAIN

IT is a common delusion of those who discuss contemporary literature that there is such an entity as the " reading public," possest of a certain uniformity of taste. There is not one public; there are many publics,—as many in fact as there are different kinds of taste; and the extent of an author's popularity is in proportion to the number of these separate publics he may chance to please. Scott, for example, appealed not only to those who relished romance and enjoyed excitement, but also to those who appreciated his honest portrayal of sturdy characters. Thackeray is preferred by ambitious youths who are insidiously flattered by his tacit compliments to their knowledge of the world, by the disenchanted who cannot help seeing the petty meannesses of society, and by the less sophisticated in whom sentiment has not gone to seed in sentimentality. Dickens in his own day bid for the approval of those who liked broad caricature (and were, therefore, pleased with Stiggins and Chadband), of those who fed greedily on plentiful pathos (and were, therefore, delighted with the death-beds of Smike and Paul Dombey and Little Nell) and also of those who asked for unexpected adventure (and were, therefore, glad to disentangle the melodramatic intrigues of Ralph Nickleby).

In like manner the American author who has chosen to call himself Mark Twain has attained to an immense popularity because the qualities he possesses in a high degree appeal to so many and so widely varied publics,—first of all, no doubt, to the public that revels in hearty and robust fun, but also to the public which is glad to be swept along by the full current of adventure, which is sincerely touched by manly pathos, which is satisfied by vigorous and exact portrayal of character, which respects shrewdness and wisdom and sanity and which appreciates a healthy hatred of pretense and affectation and sham. Perhaps no one book of Mark Twain's—with the possible exception of ' Huckleberry Finn '—is equally a favorite with all his readers; and perhaps some of his best characteristics are absent from his earlier books or but doubtfully latent in them. Mark Twain is many-sided; and he has ripened in knowledge and in power since he first attracted attention as a wild Western funny man. As he has grown older he has reflected more; he has both broadened and deepened. The writer of "comic copy" for a mining-camp newspaper has developed into a liberal humorist, handling life seriously and making his readers think as he makes them laugh, until to-day Mark Twain has perhaps the largest audience of any author now using the English language. To trace the stages of this evolution and to count the steps whereby the sage-brush reporter has risen to the rank of a writer of world-wide celebrity, is as interesting as it is instructive.

I

SAMUEL LANGHORNE CLEMENS was born November 30, 1835, at Florida, Missouri. His father was a merchant who had come from Tennessee and who removed soon after his son's birth to Hannibal, a little town on the Mississippi. What Hannibal was like and what were the circumstances of Mr. Clemens's boyhood we can see for ourselves in the convincing pages of 'Tom Sawyer.' Mr. Howells has called Hannibal "a loafing, out-at-elbows, down-at-the-heels, slaveholding Mississippi town"; and the elder Clemens was himself a slave-owner, who silently abhorred slavery.

When the future author was but twelve his father died, and the son had to get his education as best he could. Of actual schooling he got little and of book-learning still less; but life itself is not a bad teacher for a boy who wants to study, and young Clemens did not waste his chances. He spent three years in the printing office of the little local paper,—for, like not a few others on the list of American authors that stretches from Benjamin Franklin to William Dean Howells, he began his connection with literature by setting type. As a journeyman printer the lad wandered from town to town and rambled even as far east as New York.

When he was seventeen he went back to the home of his boyhood resolved to become a pilot on the Mississippi. How he learnt the river he has told us in 'Life on the Mississippi,' wherein his adventures, his experiences, and his impressions while he was a cub-pilot are recorded with a combination of precise veracity and abundant humor which makes the earlier chapters of that marvelous book a most masterly fragment of autobiography. The life of a pilot was full of interest and excitement and opportunity, and what young Clemens saw and heard and divined during the years when he was going up and down the mighty river we may read in the pages of 'Huckleberry Finn' and 'Pudd'nhead Wilson.' But toward the end of the fifties the railroads began to rob the river of its supremacy as a carrier; and in the beginning of the sixties the Civil War broke out and the Mississippi no longer went unvext to the sea. The skill, slowly and laboriously acquired, was suddenly rendered useless, and at twenty-five the young man found himself bereft of his calling. As a border state, Missouri was sending her sons into the armies of the Union and into the armies of the Confederacy, while many a man stood doubting, not knowing which way to turn. The ex-pilot has given us the record of his very brief and inglorious service as a soldier of the South. When this escapade was swiftly ended, he went to the northwest with his brother, who had been appointed lieutenant-governor of Nevada. Thus the man who had been born on the borderland of North and South, who had gone East as a jour printer, who had been again and again up and down the Mississippi, now went West while he was still plastic and impressionable; and he had thus another chance to increase that intimate knowledge of American life and American character which is one of the most precious of his possessions.

While still on the river he had written a satiric letter or two signed "Mark Twain"—taking the name from a call of the man who heaves the lead and who cries "By the mark, three," "Mark twain," and so on. In Nevada he went to the mines and lived the life he has described in 'Roughing It,' but when he failed to "strike it rich," he naturally drifted into journalism and back into a newspaper office again. The 'Virginia City Enterprise' was not overmanned, and the new-comer did all sorts of odd jobs, finding time now and then to write a sketch which seemed important enough to permit of his signature. The name of Mark Twain soon began to be known to those who were curious in newspaper humor. After a while he was drawn across the mountains to San Francisco, where he found casual employment on the 'Morning Call,' and where he joined himself to a little group of aspiring literators which included Bret Harte, Noah Brooks, Charles Henry Webb, and Mr. Charles Warren Stoddart.

It was in 1867 that Webb published Mark Twain's first book, the 'Celebrated Jumping Frog of Calaveras'; and it was in 1867 that the proprietors of the 'Alta California' supplied him with the funds necessary to enable him to become one of the passengers on the steamer *Quaker City*, which had been chartered to take a select party on what is now known as the Mediterranean trip. The weekly letters, in which he set forth what befell him on this journey, were printed in the 'Alta' Sunday after Sunday, and were copied freely by the other Californian papers. These letters served as the foundation of a book published in 1869 and called the 'Innocents Abroad,' a book which instantly brought to the author celebrity and cash.

Both of these valuable aids to ambition were increased by his next step, his appearance on the lecture platform. Noah Brooks, who was present at his first attempt, has recorded that Mark Twain's "method as a lecturer was distinctly unique and novel. His slow, deliberate drawl, the anxious and perturbed expression of his visage, the apparently painful effort with which he framed his sentences, the surprize that spread over his face when the audience roared with delight or rapturously applauded the finer passages of his word-painting, were unlike anything of the kind they had ever known." In the many years since that first appearance the method has not changed, altho it has probably matured. Mark Twain is one of the most effective of platform-speakers and one of the most artistic, with an art of his own which is very individual and very elaborate in spite of its seeming simplicity.

Altho he succeeded abundantly as a lecturer, and altho he was the author of the most widely-circulated book of the decade, Mark Twain still thought of himself only as a journalist; and when he gave up the West for the East, he became an editor of the ' Buffalo Express,' in which he had bought an interest. In 1870 he married;

and it is perhaps not indiscreet to remark that his was another of those happy unions of which there have been so many in the annals of American authorship. In 1871 he removed to Hartford, which was to be his home for thirty years; and at the same time he gave up newspaper work.

In 1872 he wrote 'Roughing It,' and in the following year came his first sustained attempt at fiction, the 'Gilded Age,' written in collaboration with Charles Dudley Warner. The character of Colonel Mulberry Sellers Mark Twain soon took out of this book to make it the central figure of a play, which the late John T. Raymond acted hundreds of times thruout the United States, the playgoing public pardoning the inexpertness of the dramatist in favor of the delicious humor and the compelling veracity with which the chief character was presented. So universal was this type and so broadly recognizable its traits that there were many towns in which someone accosted the actor who impersonated the ever-hopeful schemer with the declaration: "I 'm the original of *Sellers!* Did n't Mark ever tell you? Well, he took the *Colonel* from me!"

Encouraged by the welcome accorded to this first attempt at fiction, Mark Twain turned to the days of his boyhood and wrote 'Tom Sawyer,' published in 1875. He also collected his sketches, scattered here and there in newspapers

and magazines.   Toward the end of the seventies
he went to Europe again with his family; and
the result of this journey is recorded in 'A Tramp
Abroad,' published in 1880.   Another volume of
sketches, the 'Stolen White Elephant,' was put
forth in 1882; and in the same year Mark Twain
first came forward as a historical novelist—if the
'Prince and the Pauper' can fairly be called a historical novel.   The year after he sent forth the
volume describing his 'Life on the Mississippi';
and in 1884 he followed this with the story in
which that life has been crystallized forever,
'Huckleberry Finn,' the finest of his books, the
deepest in its insight, and the widest in its appeal.

This Odyssey of the Mississippi was published
by a new firm, in which the author was a chief
partner, just as Sir Walter Scott had been an asso-
ciate of Ballantyne and Constable.   There was at
first a period of prosperity in which the house
issued the 'Personal Memoirs' of Grant, giving
his widow checks for $350,000 in 1886, and in
which Mark Twain himself published 'A Connecticut Yankee at King Arthur's Court,' a volume of 'Merry Tales,' and a story called the
'American Claimant,' wherein Colonel Sellers
reappears.   Then there came a succession of hard
years; and at last the publishing-house in which
Mark Twain was a partner failed, as the publishing-house in which Walter Scott was a partner

had formerly failed. The author of 'Huckleberry Finn' was past sixty when he found himself suddenly saddled with a load of debt, just as the author of 'Waverley' had been burdened full threescore years earlier; and Mark Twain stood up stoutly under it as Scott had done before him. More fortunate than the Scotchman, the American lived to pay the debt in full.

Since the disheartening crash came, he has given to the public a third Mississippi River tale, 'Pudd'nhead Wilson,' issued in 1894; and a third historical novel, 'Joan of Arc,' a reverent and sympathetic study of the bravest figure in all French history, printed anonymously in 'Harper's Magazine' and then in a volume acknowledged by the author in 1896. As one of the results of a lecturing tour around the world he prepared another volume of travels, 'Following the Equator,' published toward the end of 1897. Mention must also be made of a fantastic tale called 'Tom Sawyer Abroad,' sent forth in 1894, of a volume of sketches, the 'Million Pound Bank-Note,' assembled in 1893, and also of a collection of literary essays, 'How to Tell a Story,' published in 1897.

This is but the barest outline of Mark Twain's life,—such a brief summary as we must have before us if we wish to consider the conditions under which the author has developed and the stages of his growth. It will serve, however, to show how various have been his forms of activity,—printer, pilot, miner, journalist, traveler, lecturer, novelist, publisher,—and to suggest the width of his experience of life.

II

A HUMORIST is often without honor in his own country. Perhaps this is partly because humor is likely to be familiar, and familiarity breeds contempt. Perhaps it is partly because (for some strange reason) we tend to despise those who make us laugh, while we respect those who make us weep—forgetting that there are formulas for forcing tears quite as facile as the formulas for forcing smiles. Whatever the reason, the fact is indisputable that the humorist must pay the penalty of his humor, he must run the risk of being tolerated as a mere fun-maker, not to be taken seriously, and not worthy of critical consideration. This penalty has been paid by Mark Twain. In many of the discussions of American literature he has been dismist as tho he were only a competitor of his predecessors, Artemus Ward and John Phœnix, instead of being, what he is really, a writer who is to be classed—at whatever interval only time may decide—rather with Cervantes and Molière.

Like the heroines of the problem-plays of the modern theater, Mark Twain has had to live down his past. His earlier writing gave but little promise of the enduring qualities obvious enough in his later works. Noah Brooks has told us how he was advised if he wisht to "see genuine specimens of American humor, frolicsome, extravagant, and audacious," to look up the sketches which the then almost unknown Mark Twain was printing in a Nevada newspaper. The humor of Mark Twain is still American, still frolicsome, extravagant, and audacious; but it is riper now and richer, and it has taken unto itself other qualities existing only in germ in these firstlings of his muse. The sketches in the 'Jumping Frog' and the letters which made up the 'Innocents Abroad' are "comic copy," as the phrase is in newspaper offices—comic copy not altogether unlike what John Phœnix had written and Artemus Ward,—better indeed than the work of these newspaper humorists (for Mark Twain had it in him to develop as they did not), but not essentially dissimilar.

And in the eyes of many who do not think for themselves, Mark Twain was only the author of these genuine specimens of American humor. For when the public has once made up its mind about any man's work, it does not relish any attempt to force it to unmake this opinion and to remake it. Like other juries, it does not like to be ordered to reconsider its verdict as contrary to the facts of the case. It is always sluggish in beginning the necessary readjustment, and not only sluggish, but somewhat grudging. Naturally it cannot help seeing the later works of a popular writer from the point of view it had to take to enjoy his earlier writings. And thus the author of ' Huckleberry Finn ' and ' Joan of Arc ' was forced to pay a high price for the early and abundant popularity of the ' Innocents Abroad.'

No doubt, a few of his earlier sketches were inexpensive in their elements; made of materials worn threadbare by generations of earlier funny men, they were sometimes cut in the pattern of his predecessors. No doubt, some of the earliest of all were crude and highly colored, and may even be called forced, not to say violent. No doubt, also, they did not suggest the seriousness and the melancholy which always must underlie the deepest humor, as we find it in Cervantes and Molière, in Swift and in Lowell. But even a careless reader, skipping thru the book in idle amusement, ought to have been able to see in the ' Innocents Abroad,' that the writer of this liveliest of books of travel was no mere merry-andrew, grinning thru a horse-collar to make sport for the groundlings; but a sincere observer of life, seeing thru his own eyes and setting down

what he saw with abundant humor, of course,
but also with profound respect for the eternal
verities.

George Eliot in one of her essays calls those
who parody lofty themes "debasers of the moral
currency." Mark Twain is always an advocate
of the sterling ethical standard. He is ready to
overwhelm an affectation with irresistible laughter, but he never lacks reverence for the things
that really deserve reverence. It is not at the
Old Masters that he scoffs in Italy, but rather at
those who pay lip-service to things which they
neither enjoy nor understand. For a ruin or a
painting or a legend that does not seem to him
to deserve the appreciation in which it is held he
refuses to affect an admiration he does not feel;
he cannot help being honest—he was born so.
For meanness of all kinds he has a burning contempt; and on Abelard he pours out the vials of
his wrath. He has a quick eye for all humbugs
and a scorching scorn for them; but there is no
attempt at being funny in the manner of the
cockney comedians when he stands in the awful
presence of the Sphinx. He is not taken in by
the glamor of Palestine; he does not lose his head
there; he keeps his feet; but he knows that he is
standing on holy ground; and there is never a
hint of irreverence in his attitude.

'A Tramp Abroad' is a better book than the 'Innocents Abroad'; it is quite as laughter-provoking, and its manner is far more restrained. Mark Twain was then master of his method, sure of himself, secure of his popularity; and he could do his best and spare no pains to be certain that it was his best. Perhaps there is a slight falling off in 'Following the Equator'; a trace of fatigue, of weariness, of disenchantment. But the last book of travels has passages as broadly humorous as any of the first; and it proves the author's possession of a pithy shrewdness not to be suspected from a perusal of its earliest predecessor. The first book was the work of a young fellow rejoicing in his own fun and resolved to make his readers laugh with him or at him; the latest book is the work of an older man, who has found that life is not all laughter, but whose eye is as clear as ever and whose tongue is as plain-spoken.

These three books of travel are like all other books of travel in that they relate in the first person what the author went forth to see. Autobiographic also are 'Roughing It' and 'Life on the Mississippi,' and they have always seemed to me better books than the more widely circulated travels. They are better because they are the result of a more intimate knowledge of the material dealt with. Every traveler is of necessity but a bird of passage; he is a mere carpet-

bagger; his acquaintance with the countries he
visits is external only; and this acquaintance-
ship is made only when he is a full-grown
man.   But Mark Twain's knowledge of the
Mississippi was acquired in his youth; it was
not purchased with a price; it was his birthright;
and it was internal and complete.   And his
knowledge of the mining-camp was achieved in
early manhood when the mind is open and sensi-
tive to every new impression.   There is in both
these books a fidelity to the inner truth, a certainty of touch, a sweep of vision, not to be
found in the three books of travels.   For my
own part I have long thought that Mark Twain
could securely rest his right to survive as an
author on those opening chapters in 'Life on
the Mississippi' in which he makes clear the
difficulties, the seeming impossibilities, that
fronted those who wisht to learn the
river.   These chapters are bold and brilliant;
and they picture for us forever a period and a set
of conditions, singularly interesting and splen-
didly varied, that otherwise would have had to
forego all adequate record.

III

It is highly probable that when an author reveals the power of evoking views of places and

of calling up portraits of people such as Mark Twain showed in 'Life on the Mississippi,' and when he has the masculine grasp of reality Mark Twain made evident in 'Roughing It,' he must needs sooner or later turn from mere fact to avowed fiction and become a story-teller. The long stories which Mark Twain has written fall into two divisions,—first, those of which the scene is laid in the present, in reality, and mostly in the Mississippi Valley, and second, those of which the scene is laid in the past, in fantasy mostly, and in Europe.

As my own liking is a little less for the latter group, there is no need for me now to linger over them. In writing these tales of the past Mark Twain was making up stories in his head; personally I prefer the tales of his in which he has his foot firm on reality. The 'Prince and the Pauper' has the essence of boyhood in it; it has variety and vigor; it has abundant humor and plentiful pathos; and yet I for one would give the whole of it for the single chapter in which Tom Sawyer lets the contract for white-washing his aunt's fence.

Mr. Howells has declared that there are two kinds of fiction he likes almost equally well,—" a real novel and a pure romance "; and he joyfully accepts 'A Connecticut Yankee at King Arthur's Court' as "one of the greatest romances ever

imagined." It is a humorous romance overflow-
ing with stalwart fun; and it is not irreverent but
iconoclastic, in that it breaks not a few disestablished idols. It is intensely American and intensely nineteenth century and intensely democratic—in the best sense of that abused adjective.
The British critics were greatly displeased with
the book:—and we are reminded of the fact that
the Spanish still somewhat resent ' Don Quixote '
because it brings out too truthfully the fatal gap
in the Spanish character between the ideal and
the real. So much of the feudal still survives in
British society that Mark Twain's merry and
elucidating assault on the past seemed to some
almost an insult to the present.

But no critic, British or American, has ventured
to discover any irreverence in ' Joan of Arc,'
wherein indeed the tone is almost devout and the
humor almost too much subdued. Perhaps it is
my own distrust of the so-called historical novel,
my own disbelief that it can ever be anything but
an inferior form of art, which makes me care less
for this worthy effort to honor a noble figure.
And elevated and dignified as is the ' Joan of Arc,'
I do not think that it shows us Mark Twain at
his best; altho it has many a passage that only
he could have written, it is perhaps the least
characteristic of his works. Yet it may well be
that the certain measure of success he has achieved

in handling a subject so lofty and so serious, helped to open the eyes of the public to see the solid merits of his other stories, in which his humor has fuller play and in which his natural gifts are more abundantly displayed.

Of these other stories three are " real novels," to use Mr. Howells's phrase; they are novels as real as any in any literature. ' Tom Sawyer' and 'Huckleberry Finn' and 'Pudd'nhead Wilson' are invaluable contributions to American literature—for American literature is nothing if it is not a true picture of American life and if it does not help us to understand ourselves. ' Huckleberry Finn' is a very amusing volume, and a generation has read its pages and laughed over it immoderately; but it is very much more than a funny book; it is a marvelously accurate portrayal of a whole civilization. Mr. Ormsby, in an essay which accompanies his translation of ' Don Quixote,' has pointed out that for a full century after its publication that greatest of novels was enjoyed chiefly as a tale of humorous misadventure, and that three generations had laughed over it before anybody suspected that it was more than a mere funny book. It is perhaps rather with the picaresque romances of Spain that ' Huckleberry Finn ' is to be compared than with the masterpiece of Cervantes; but I do not think that it will be a century or that it will take three generations before we Americans generally discover how great a book 'Huckleberry Finn' really is, how keen its vision of character, how close its observation of life, how sound its philosophy, and how it records for us once and for all certain phases of southwestern society which it is most important for us to perceive and to understand. The influence of slavery, the prevalence of feuds, the conditions and the circumstances that make lynching possible—all these things are set before us clearly and without comment. It is or us to draw our own moral, each for himself, as we do when we see Shakspere acted.

'Huckleberry Finn,' in its art, for one thing, and also in its broader range, is superior to 'Tom Sawyer' and to 'Pudd'nhead Wilson,' fine as both these are in their several ways. In no book in our language, to my mind, has the boy, simply as a boy, been better realized than in 'Tom Sawyer.' In some respects 'Pudd'nhead Wilson' is the most dramatic of Mark Twain's longer stories, and also the most ingenious; like 'Tom Sawyer' and 'Huckleberry Finn,' it has the full flavor of the Mississippi River, on which its author spent his own boyhood, and from contact with the soil of which he has always risen reinvigorated.

It is by these three stories, and especially by 'Huckleberry Finn,' that Mark Twain is likely to live longest. Nowhere else is the life of the Mississippi Valley so truthfully recorded. Nowhere else can we find a gallery of southwestern characters as varied and as veracious as those Huck Finn met in his wanderings. The histories of literature all praise the 'Gil Blas' of Le Sage for its amusing adventures, its natural characters, its pleasant humor, and its insight into human frailty; and the praise is deserved. But in every one of these qualities 'Huckleberry Finn' is superior to 'Gil Blas.' Le Sage set the model of the picaresque novel, and Mark Twain followed his example; but the American book is richer than the French—deeper, finer, stronger. It would be hard to find in any language better specimens of pure narrative, better examples of the power of telling a story and of calling up action so that the reader cannot help but see it, than Mark Twain's account of the Shepardson-Grangerford feud, and his description of the shooting of Boggs by Sherbourn and of the foiled attempt to lynch Sherbourn afterward.

These scenes, fine as they are, vivid, powerful, and most artistic in their restraint, can be matched in the two other books. In 'Tom Sawyer' they can be paralleled by the chapter in which the boy and the girl are lost in the cave, and Tom, seeing a gleam of light in the distance, discovers that it is a candle carried by Indian Joe,

MARK TWAIN

the one enemy he has in the world. In 'Pudd'n-
head Wilson' the great passages of 'Huckleberry Finn' are rivaled by that most pathetic
account of the weak son willing to sell his own
mother as a slave "down the river."   Altho no
one of the books is sustained thruout on this
high level, and altho, in truth, there are in each
of them passages here and there that we could
wish away (because they are not worthy of the
association in which we find them), I have no
hesitation in expressing here my own conviction
that the man who has given us four scenes like
these is to be compared with the masters of
literature; and that he can abide the comparison
with equanimity.

IV

PERHAPS I myself prefer these three Mississippi
Valley books above all Mark Twain's other
writings (altho with no lack of affection for
those also) partly because these have the most
of the flavor of the soil about them.   After veracity and the sense of the universal, what I
best relish in literature is this native aroma,
pungent, homely, and abiding.   Yet I feel sure
that I should not rate him so high if he were
the author of these three books only.   They are
the best of him, but the others are good also, and

good in a different way. Other writers have given us this local color more or less artistically, more or less convincingly: one New England and another New York, a third Virginia, and a fourth Georgia, and a fifth Wisconsin; but who so well as Mark Twain has given us the full spectrum of the Union? With all his exactness in reproducing the Mississippi Valley, Mark Twain is not sectional in his outlook; he is national always. He is not narrow; he is not western or eastern; he is American with a certain largeness and boldness and freedom and certainty that we like to think of as befitting a country so vast as ours and a people so independent.

In Mark Twain we have "the national spirit as seen with our own eyes," declared Mr. Howells; and, from more points of view than one, Mark Twain seems to me to be the very embodiment of Americanism. Self-educated in the hard school of life, he has gone on broadening his outlook as he has grown older. Spending many years abroad, he has come to understand other nationalities, without enfeebling his own native faith. Combining a mastery of the commonplace with an imaginative faculty, he is a practical idealist. No respecter of persons, he has a tender regard for his fellowman. Irreverent toward all outworn superstitions, he has ever

revealed the deepest respect for all things truly
worthy of reverence. Unwilling to take pay in
words, he is impatient always to get at the root
of the matter, to pierce to the center, to see the
thing as it is. He has a habit of standing up-
right, of thinking for himself, and of hitting hard
at whatsoever seems to him hateful and mean;
but at the core of him there is genuine gentle-
ness and honest sympathy, brave humanity and
sweet kindliness. Perhaps it is boastful for us
to think that these characteristics which we
see in Mark Twain are characteristics also of the
American people as a whole; but it is pleasant
to think so.

Mark Twain has the very marrow of Americanism. He is as intensely and as typically
American as Franklin or Emerson or Hawthorne.
He has not a little of the shrewd common-sense
and the homely and unliterary directness of Franklin. He is not without a share of the aspiration
and the elevation of Emerson; and he has a philosophy of his own as optimistic as Emerson's.
He possesses also somewhat of Hawthorne's interest in ethical problems, with something of the
same power of getting at the heart of them; he,
too, has written his parables and apologs
wherein the moral is obvious and unobtruded.
He is uncompromisingly honest; and his conscience is as rugged as his style sometimes is.

No American author has to-day at his command a style more nervous, more varied, more flexible, or more direct than Mark Twain's. His colloquial ease should not hide from us his mastery of all the devices of rhetoric. He may seem to disobey the letter of the law sometimes, but he is always obedient to the spirit. He never speaks unless he has something to say; and then he says it tersely, sharply, with a freshness of epithet and an individuality of phrase always accurate, however unacademic. His vocabulary is enormous, and it is deficient only in the dead words; his language is alive always, and actually tingling with vitality. He rejoices in the daring noun and in the audacious adjective. His instinct for the exact word is not always assured, and now and again he has failed to exercise it ; but we do not find in his prose the flatting and sharping he censured in Fenimore Cooper's. His style has none of the cold perfection of an antique statue; it is too modern and too American for that, and too completely the expression of the man himself, sincere and straightforward. It is not free from slang, altho this is far less frequent than one might expect; but it does its work swiftly and cleanly. And it is capable of immense variety. Consider the tale of the Blue Jay in ' A Tramp Abroad,' wherein the humor is sustained by unstated pathos; what could be better told than this, with every word the right word and in the right place? And take Huck Finn's description of the storm when he was alone on the island, which is in dialect, which will not parse, which bristles with double negatives, but which none the less is one of the finest passages of descriptive prose in all American literature.

V

AFTER all, it is as a humorist pure and simple that Mark Twain is best known and best beloved. In the preceding pages I have tried to point out the several ways in which he transcends humor, as the word is commonly restricted, and to show that he is no mere fun-maker. But he is a fun-maker beyond all question, and he has made millions laugh as no other man of our century has done. The laughter he has aroused is wholesome and self-respecting; it clears the atmosphere. For this we cannot but be grateful. As Lowell said, "let us not be ashamed to confess that, if we find the tragedy a bore, we take the profoundest satisfaction in the farce. It is a mark of sanity." There is no laughter in Don Quixote, the noble enthusiast whose wits are unsettled; and there is little on the lips of *Alceste*, the misanthrope of Molière; but for both of them life would have been easier had they known how to laugh. Cervantes himself, and Molière also, found relief in laughter for their melancholy; and it was the sense of humor which kept them tolerantly interested in the spectacle of humanity, altho life had prest hardly on them both. On Mark Twain also life has left its scars; but he has bound up his wounds and battled forward with a stout heart, as Cervantes did, and Molière. It was Molière who declared that it was a strange business to undertake to make people laugh; but even now, after two centuries, when the best of Molière's plays are acted, mirth breaks out again and laughter overflows.

It would be doing Mark Twain a disservice to compare him to Molière, the greatest comic dramatist of all time; and yet there is more than one point of similarity. Just as Mark Twain began by writing comic copy which contained no prophesy of a masterpiece like 'Huckleberry Finn,' so Molière was at first the author only of semi-acrobatic farces on the Italian model in no wise presaging 'Tartuffe' and the 'Misanthrope.' Just as Molière succeeded first of all in pleasing the broad public that likes robust fun, and then slowly and step by step developed into a dramatist who set on the stage enduring figures plucked out of the abounding life about him, so also has Mark Twain grown, ascending from the 'Jumping Frog' to 'Huckleberry Finn,' as comic as its elder brotner and as laughter-provoking, but charged also with meaning and with philosophy. And like Molière again, Mark Twain has kept solid hold of the material world; his doctrine is not of the earth earthy, but it is never sublimated into sentimentality. He sympathizes with the spiritual side of humanity, while never ignoring the sensual. Like Molière, Mark Twain takes his stand on common-sense and thinks scorn of affectation of every sort. He understands sinners and strugglers and weaklings; and he is not harsh with them, reserving his scorching hatred for hypocrites and pretenders and frauds.

At how long an interval Mark Twain shall be rated after Molière and Cervantes it is for the future to declare. All that we can see clearly now is that it is with them that he is to be classed,— with Molière and Cervantes, with Chaucer and Fielding, humorists all of them, and all of them manly men.

(1898.)

A NOTE ON MAUPASSANT

A NOTE ON MAUPASSANT

A STUDENT of the literature of our own time
who has only recently completed his first
half century of life cannot help feeling suddenly
aged and almost antiquated when he awakes to
the fact that he has been privileged to see the
completed literary career of two such accomplished craftsmen as Robert Louis Stevenson and
Guy de Maupassant. In youth they were full
of promise, and in maturity they were rich in
performance; and all too soon the lives
of both came to an end, when their powers
were still growing, when their outlook on
life was still broadening, and when they bid
fair, both of them, to bring forth many another
book riper and wiser than any they had already
given us.

The points of contrast between the two men
thus untimely taken away are as striking as the
points of similarity. Both were artists ardently
in love with the technic of their craft, delighting
in their own skill, and ever on the alert to find
new occasion for the display of their mastery of
the methods of fiction. Stevenson was a Scotch-

man; and his pseudo-friend has told us that there was in him something of "the shorter catechist." Maupassant was a Norman, and he had never given a thought to the glorifying of God. The man who wrote in English found the theme of his minor masterpieces in the conflict of which the battle-ground is the human heart. The man who wrote in French began by caring little or nothing for the heart or the soul or the mind, and by concentrating all his skill upon a record of the deeds of the human body. The one has left us 'Markheim' and the 'Strange Case of Dr. Jekyll and Mr. Hyde,' while the other made his first bid for fame with 'Boule de suif.'

In the preface of 'Pierre et Jean,' Maupassant has recorded how he acquired from Louis Bouilhet the belief that a single lyric, a scant hundred lines, would give immortality to a poet if only the work were fine enough, and that for the author who sought to escape oblivion there was only one course to pursue—to learn his trade thoroly, to master every secret of the craft, to do his best always, in the hope that some fortunate day the Muse would reward his unfailing devotion. And from Flaubert, the author of that merciless masterpiece 'Madame Bovary,' the young man learned the importance of individuality, of originality, of the personal note which

should be all his own, and which should never
suggest or recall any one else's. Flaubert was
kindly and encouraging, but he was a desperately
severe taskmaster. At Flaubert's dictation
Maupassant gave up verse for prose; and for
seven years he wrote incessantly and published
nothing. The stories and tales and verses and
dramas of those seven years of apprenticeship
were ruthlessly criticized by the author of 'Sa-
lammbô,' and then they were destroyed unprinted.
In all the long history of literature there is no
record of any other author who served so severe
a novitiate.

Douglas Jerrold once said of a certain British
author who had begun to publish very young
that "he had taken down the shutters before he
had anything to put up in the shop window."
From being transfixt by such a jibe Maupassant
was preserved by Flaubert. When he was
thirty he contributed that masterpiece of ironic
humor 'Boule de suif,' to the 'Soirées de Médan,'
a volume of short-stories put forth by the late
Émile Zola, with the collaboration of a little
group of his friends and followers. On this first
appearance in the arena of letters Maupassant
stept at once to a foremost place. That was in
1880 ; and in 1892 his mind gave way and he was
taken to the asylum, where he soon died. In
those twelve years he had published a dozen

volumes of short-stories and half a dozen novels.
Of the novel he might have made himself master
in time; of the short-story he proved himself a
master with the very earliest of all his tales.

It must be admitted at once that many of Maupassant's earlier short-stories have to do with the
lower aspects of man's merely animal activity.
Maupassant had an abundance of what the French
themselves called "Gallic salt." His humor was
not squeamish; it delighted in dealing with
themes that our Anglo-Saxon prudery prefers not
to touch. But even at the beginning this liking
of his for the sort of thing that we who speak
English prefer to avoid in print never led him to
put dirt where dirt was not a necessary element
of his narrative. Dirty many of these tales were,
no doubt; but many of them were perfectly
clean. He never went out of his way to offend,
as not a few of his compatriots seem to enjoy
doing. He handled whatever subject he took
with the same absolute understanding of its value,
of the precise treatment best suited to it. If it
was a dirty theme he had chosen—and he had no
prejudice against such a theme—he did whatever
was needful to get the most out of his subject.
If it was not a dirty theme, then there was never
any touch of the tar-brush. Whenever the subject itself was inoffensive his treatment was also
immaculate. There is never any difficulty in

making a choice out of his hundred or two brief
tales; and it is easy to pick out a dozen or a score
of his short-stories needing absolutely no expur-
gation, because they are wholly free from any
phrase or any suggestion likely to bring the blush
of shame to the cheek of innocence.   In matters
of taste, as we Anglo-Saxons regard them, Maupassant was a man without prejudices.   But he
was a man also of immitigable veracity in his
dealing with the material of his art, in his handling of life itself.   He told the truth as it was given
to him to see the truth; not the whole truth, of
course, for it is given to no man to see that.   His
artistic standard was lofty; and he did his best
not to lie about life.   And in some ways this veracity of his may be accepted, if not as an equivalent for morality, at least as a not wholly unworthy substitute.

The most of Maupassant's earlier tales were not
a little hard and stern and unsympathetic; and
here again Maupassant was the disciple of Flaubert.   His manner was not only unemotional at
first, it was icily impassive.   These first stories
of his were cold and they were contemptuous;—
at least they made the reader feel that the author
heartily despised the pitiable and pitiful creatures
he was depicting.   They dealt mainly with the
externals of life,—with outward actions; and
the internal motives of the several actors were

not always adequately implied. But in time the mind came to interest Maupassant as much as the body. In the beginning he seems to have considered solely what his characters did, and he cared little to tell us what they felt and what they thought ; probably he did not know himself and did not try to know.

The inquirers who should read his stories in the strict sequence of their production could not fail to be struck with the first awakening of his curiosity about human feeling; and they might easily trace the steady growth of his interest in psychologic states. Telling us at first bluntly and barely what his characters did, he came in time to find his chief pleasure in suggesting to us not only what they felt, but especially what they vaguely feared. Toward the end of his brief career the thought of death and the dread of mental disease seemed to possess him more and more with a haunting horror that kept recurring with a pathetic persistence. He came to have a close terror of death, almost an obsession of the grave; and to find a parallel to this we should have to go back four hundred years, to Villon, also a realist and a humorist with a profound relish for the outward appearances of life. But Maupassant went far beyond the earlier poet, and he even developed a fondness for the morbid and the abnormal. This is revealed in 'Le Horla,'

174

the appalling story in which he took for his own
Fitzjames O'Brien's uncanny monster, invisible,
and yet tangible. In the hands of the clever
Irish-American this tale had been gruesome
enough; but the Frenchman was able to give it
an added touch of terror by making the unfortunate victim discover that the creature he feared
had a stronger will than his own and that he was
being hypnotized to his doom by a being whom he
could not see, but whose presence he could feel.
There is more than one of these later tales in
which we seem to perceive the premonition of
the madness which came upon Maupassant before his death.

At first he was an observer only, a recorder of
the outward facts of average humanity. He had
no theories about life, or even about art. He had
no ideas of his own, no general ideas, no interest
in ideas. He did not care to talk about technic
or even about his own writings. He put on
paper what he had seen, the peasants of Normandy, the episodes of the war, the nether-world
of the newspaper. He cared nothing for morality,
but he was unfailingly veracious, never falsifying
the facts of existence as he had seen it himself.
Then, at the end, it is not what his characters do
that most interested him, not what they are, not
what they think, but what they feel, and, above
all, what they fear.

In every work of art there are at least four elements, which we may separate if we wish to consider each of them in turn. First of all, there is the technic of the author, his craftsmanship, his mastery of the tools of his trade; and by almost universal consent Maupassant is held to be one of the master craftsmen of the short-story. Second, there is the amount of observation of life which the author reveals; and here again Maupassant takes rank among the leaders, altho the sphere in which he observed had its marked limitations and its obvious exclusions. Thirdly, there is the underlying and informing imagination which invents and relates and sustains; and there is no disputing the vigor of Maupassant's imagination, altho it was not lofty and altho it lacked variety. Finally, there is always to be taken into account what one may term the author's philosophy of life, his attitude toward the common problems of humanity; and here it is that Maupassant is most lacking,—for his opinions are negligible and his attempts at intellectual speculation are of slight value.

Technic can be acquired; and Maupassant had studied at the feet of that master technician Flaubert. Observation can be trained; and Maupassant had deliberately developed his power of vision. Imagination may be stimulated by constant endeavor to a higher achievement; and

Maupassant's ambitions were ever tending upward. Philosophy, however, is dependent upon the sum total of a man's faculties, upon his training, upon his temperament, upon the essential elements of his character; and Maupassant was not a sound thinker, and his attitude toward life is not that by which he can best withstand the adverse criticism of posterity. Primarily, he was not a thinker any more than Hugo was a thinker, or Dickens. He was only an artist—an artist in fiction; and an artist is not called upon to be a thinker, altho the supreme artists seem nearly all of them to have been men of real intellectual force.

(1902.)

THE MODERN NOVEL AND THE
MODERN PLAY

THE MODERN NOVEL AND THE
MODERN PLAY

AS we glance down the long history of literature, we cannot but remark that certain
literary forms, the novel at one time and the
drama at another, have achieved a sweeping
popularity, seemingly out of all proportion to
their actual merit at the moment when they were
flourishing most luxuriantly. In these periods
of undue expansion, the prevalent form absorbed
many talents not naturally attracted toward it.
In the beginning of the sixteenth century in
England, for instance, the drama was more
profitable, and, therefore, more alluring, than any
other field of literary endeavor; and so it was
that many a young fellow of poetic temperament
adventured himself in the rude theater of those
spacious days, even tho his native gift was only
doubtfully dramatic. No reader of Peele's plays
and of Greene's can fail to feel that these two
gentle poets were, neither of them, born play-
makers called to the stage by irresistible vocation.
Two hundred years later, after Steele and Addison
had set the pattern of the eighteenth-century

essay, the drama was comparatively neglected, and every man of letters was found striving for the unattainable ease and charm of the 'Tatler' and the 'Spectator.' Even the elephantine Johnson, congenitally incapable of airy nothings and prone always to "make little fishes talk like whales," disported ponderously in the 'Idler' and the 'Rambler.' The vogue of the essay was fleeting also; and a century later it was followed by the vogue of the novel,—a vogue which has already endured longer than that of the essay, and which has not yet shown any signs of abating. Yet the history of literature reminds us that the literary form most in favor in one century is very likely to drop out of fashion in the next; and we are justified in asking ourselves whether the novel is to be supreme in the twentieth century as it was in the nineteenth, or whether its popularity must surely wane like that of the essay.

Altho the art of fiction must be almost as old as mankind itself, the prose novel, as we know it now, is a thing of yesterday only. It is not yet a hundred years since it established itself and claimed equality with the other forms of literature. Novelists there had been, no doubt, and of the highest rank; but it was not until after 'Waverley' and its successors swept across Europe triumphant and overwhelming that a fiction in prose was admitted to full citizenship in the republic of letters. Nowadays, we are so accustomed to the novel and so familiar with its luxuriance in every modern language that we often forget its comparative youth. Yet we know that no one of the muses of old was assigned to the fostering of prose-fiction, a form of literary endeavor which the elder Greeks did not foresee. If we accept Fielding's contention that the history of 'Tom Jones' must be considered as a prose-epic, we are justified in the belief that the muse of the epic-poetry is not now without fit occupation.

Indeed, the modern novel is not only the heir of the epic, it has also despoiled the drama, the lyric and the oration of part of their inheritance. The 'Scarlet Letter,' for example, has not a little of the lofty largeness and of the stately move-ment of true tragedy; 'Paul and Virginia,' again, abounds in a passionate self-revelation which is essentially lyric; and many a novel-with-a-pur-pose, needless to name here, displays its author's readiness to avail himself of all the devices of the orator. In fact, the novel is now so various and so many-sided that its hospitality is limitless. It welcomes alike the exotic eroticism of M. Pierre Loti and the cryptic cleverness of Mr. Henry James, the accumulated adventure of Dumas and the inexorable veracity of Tolstoi. It has tempted many a man who had no native endowment for it; Motley and Parkman and Froude risked themselves in imaginative fiction, as well as in the sterner history which was their real birthright. And so did Brougham, far more unfitted for prose-fiction than Johnson was for the graceful eighteenth-century essay or than Peele and Greene were for the acted drama. Perhaps it is a consequence of this variety of method, which lets prose-fiction proffer itself to every passer-by, that we recognize in the Victorian novel the plasticity of form and the laxity of structure which we have discovered to be characteristic of the Elizabethan drama.

In her encroaching on the domain of the other muses, the prose-epic has annexed far more from her comic and tragic sisters than from any of the other six. An opportunity for a most interesting inquiry awaits the alert scholar who shall undertake to tell the rivalry of the novel and the play, tracing their influence on each other and making a catalog of their mutual borrowings. Altho the record has no special significance, it may be noted that they have never hesitated to filch plots from each other, the playwrights appropriating the inventions of the novelists and the novelists levying on the works of the playwrights, —Shakspere, the dramatist, finding the action of his ' As You Like It ' ready to his hand in a tale of Lodge's, and Le Sage, the story-teller, in his 'Gil Blas' availing himself of scenes from Spanish comedies.

Far deeper, however, than any purloining of material are other interrelations of the novel and the play, which have been continually influencing one another, even when there was no hint of any plagiarism of subject-matter. The older of the two, the drama, long served as the model of prose-fiction; and not a few of the earlier practitioners of the later art began their literary careers as writers for the theater,—Le Sage for one, and, for another, Fielding. It is not to be wondered at that they were inclined to approach the novel a little as tho it were a play, and to set their characters in motion with only a bare and summary indication of the appropriate environment. They were inclined to follow the swift methods proper enough on the stage, if not absolutely necessary there, instead of developing for themselves the more leisurely movement appropriate to prose-fiction. Both Fielding and Le Sage, it may be well to note, had profited greatly by their careful study of Molière and of his logical method of presenting character. In the 'Princess of Cleves,' —perhaps the first effort at feminine psychology in fiction,—we discover the obvious impress of both Corneille and Racine on Madame de Lafayette,—the stiffening of the will to resolute self-sacrifice of the elder dramatist and the subtler analysis of motive dexterously attempted by the younger and more tender tragic poet.

Just as Beaumarchais in the eighteenth century found his profit in a study of Le Sage's satiric attitude, so Augier in the nineteenth century, and still more, Dumas *fils*, responded to the sharp stimulus of Balzac. The richer and far more complicated presentation of character which delights and amazes us in the 'Human Comedy' was most suggestive to the younger generation of French dramatists; and no one can fail to see the reflection of Balzac in the 'Maître Guérin' of Augier and in the 'Ami des femmes' of Dumas. And, in their turn, these plays and their fellows supplied a pattern to the novelist—to Daudet especially. A certain lack of largeness, a certain artificiality of action in Daudet's 'Fromont jeune et Risler aîné,' is probably to be ascribed to the fact that the story was first conceived in the form of a play, altho it was actually written as a novel.

The British novelist with whom this French novelist is often compared, and with whom he had much in common, was also impressed profoundly by the theater of his own time and of his own country. But Dickens was less fortunate than Daudet, in that the contemporary English stage did not afford a model as worthy of imitation as the contemporary French stage. Of course, the native genius of Dickens is indisputable, but his artistic ideals are painfully unsatisfactory. His letters show him forever straining after effects for their own sake only, and striving to put just so much humor and just so much pathos into each one of the successive monthly parts into which his stories were chopped up. Very fond of the theater from his early youth, Dickens had come near going on the stage as an actor; and, in his search for effects, he borrowed inexpensive mysteries from contemporary melodrama, and he took from it the implacable and inexplicable villain ever involved in dark plottings. It is significant that 'No Thoroughfare,' the one play of his invention which was actually produced, was performed at the Adelphi, and was discovered then not to differ widely from the other robust and high-colored melodramas ordinarily acted at that hopelessly unliterary playhouse. Daudet, altho he was not gifted with the splendid creative force of Dickens, inherited the Latin tradition of restraint and harmony and proportion; and he had before his eyes on the French stage the adroitly contrived comedies of Augier and of Dumas *fils*, models far more profitable to a novelist than the violent crudities of the Adelphi.

Perhaps there is more than a hint of ingratitude in Daudet's later disgust with the inherent limitations of the drama,—a disgust more forcibly phrased by his friends, Zola and Goncourt and

Flaubert, realists all of them, eager to capture the theater also and to rule it in their own way. In their hands, the novel was an invading conqueror; and they had the arrogance that comes from an unforeseen success. They were all eager to take possession of the playhouse, and to repeat in that new field of art the profitable victories they had gained in the library. But they declined to admit that the drama was a special art, with a method of its own. They resented bitterly the failures that followed when they refused to accept the conditions of the actual theater; and they protested shrilly against these conditions when they vainly essayed to fulfil them. " What a horrible manner of writing is that which suits the stage! " Flaubert complained to George Sand. " The ellipses, the suspensions, the interrogations must be lavished, if one wishes to have liveliness; and all these things, in themselves, are very ugly." In other words, Flaubert was concerned with the rhetoric of the written word, and he had no relish for the rhythm of spoken dialog.

These French novelists refused to perceive that the drama is, of necessity, the most democratic of the arts, since it depends, and has always depended, and must ever depend, absolutely upon the public as a whole. The strength of the drama, its immense advantage over other forms of literature, lies in this, that it must appeal to the mass of men, not to the intelligent more than to the unintelligent, not to the educated more than to the uneducated, not to any sect or clique, or cotery, but to men as men. The laws of the drama may be deduced, all of them, from this principle, that in the theater the play-maker has to interest a gathering of his own contemporaries, all sorts and conditions of men. If he cannot hold their attention, move them, sway them, control them, then he has failed frankly to do what he set out to do. And he can do this, he can make them laugh, and make them weep, make them feel, and make them think, only by accepting the conditions of the theater itself. Daudet and Zola had more of the needful understanding of their fellow creatures than Flaubert and Goncourt, more of the necessary sympathy; but they had all of them not a little of the conceit of the self-made man and they assumed the egotistic attitude of the cultivated aristocrat. It would have been well if they could have taken to heart what George Sand once wrote to Flaubert: " It seems to me that your school does not consider enough the substance of things, and that it lingers too much on the surface. By dint of seeking for form, it lets go of the fact. It addresses itself to men of cultivation. But there are, strictly speaking, no men of cultivation, for we are, first of all, men."

Because the drama was popular, these artistic aristocrats despised it. Altho they pined to succeed as play-makers, they scorned the trouble of mastering the methods of the theater. Because the drama, at its highest, attained to the loftier levels of literature, they assumed that a man of letters had no need to spy out the secrets of the stage. If they could not apply in the play the methods they had been applying skilfully and successfully in the novel, so much the worse for the play. Evidently, the drama was not literature, and the theater was no place for a literary man. The fault was not in them; it could not be, since they had regenerated the novel. It must be in the stage itself, and in the stupidity of the public.

In one of his most vigorous essays, Brunetière joined issue with this little group of French novelists, and told them sharply that they had better consider anew the theatrical practises and prejudices which seemed to them absurdly outworn, and which they disdained as born of mere chance and surviving only by tradition. He bade them ask themselves if these tricks of the trade, so to style them, were not due to the fact that the dramatist's art is a special art, having its own laws, its own conditions, its own conventions, inherent in the nature of the art itself. When they exprest their conviction that the method of the novel ought to be applicable to the play, Brunetière retorted that, if the novel was the play and if the play was the novel, then in all accuracy there would be neither novel nor play, but only a single and undivided form; and he insisted that, if as a matter of fact this single form did not actually exist, if it had divided itself, if there was such a thing as a novel and such a thing as a play, then that could be only because we go to the theater to get a specific pleasure which we cannot get in the library. The practical critic gave them the sound advice that, if they sought to succeed in the theater as they had succeeded in the library, they should study the art of the playwright, endeavoring to perceive wherein it differs from the art of the story-teller.

The points of agreement between the novel and the play are so obvious that there is some excuse for overlooking the fact that the points of disagreement are almost as numerous. It is true that, in the play as in the novel, a story is developed by means of characters whose conversation is reproduced. So the game of golf is like the game of lawn-tennis, in so far as there are in both of them balls to be placed by the aid of certain implements. But as the balls are different and as the implements are different, the two games are really not at all alike; and it is when they are played most skilfully and most strictly according to the rules that they are most unlike.

The play is least dramatic when it most closely resembles the novel, as it did in the days of Peele and Greene, whose dramas are little more than narratives presented in dialog. In the three centuries since Peele and Greene, the play and the novel have been getting further and further away from each other. Each has been steadily specializing, seeking its true self, casting out the extraneous elements proved to be useless. The novel in its highest development is now a single narrative, no longer distended and delayed by intercalated tales, such as we find in ' Don Quixote' and 'Tom Jones,' in 'Wilhelm Meister' and in 'Pickwick,' inserted for no artistic reason, but merely because the author happened to have them on hand. The play in its highest development is now a single action, swiftly presented, and kept free from lyrical and oratorical digressions existing for their own sake and not aiding in the main purpose of the drama.

The practitioners of each art conceive their stories in accordance with the necessities of that art, the novelist thinking in terms of the printed page and the dramatist thinking in terms of the actual theater, with its actors and with its spectators. Here, indeed, is a chief reason why the perspective of the play is different from the perspective of the novel, in that the playwright must perforce take account of his audience, of its likes and its dislikes, of its traditions and its desires. The novelist need not give a thought to his readers, assured that those in sympathy with his attitude and his mood will find him out sooner or later. To the story-teller, readers may come singly and at intervals; but the play-maker has to attract his audience in a mass. Much of the merely literary merit of a drama may be enjoyed by a lone reader under the library lamp; but its essential dramatic quality is completely and satisfactorily revealed only in front of the footlights when the theater is filled with spectators.

It is this consciousness that his appeal is not to any individual man, but to man in the mass, that makes the dramatist what he is. To scattered readers, each sitting alone, an author may whisper many things which he would not dare blurt out before a crowd. The playwright knows that he can never whisper slyly; he must always speak out boldly so that all may hear him; and he must phrase what he has to say so as to please the boys in the gallery without insulting the women in the stage-boxes. To the silent pressure of these unrelated spectators he responds by seeking the broadest basis for his play, by appealing to elemental human sympathy, by attempting themes with more or less of universality. It is because the drama is the most democratic of the arts that the dramatist cannot narrow himself as the novelist may, if he chooses; and it is because this breadth of appeal is inherent in the acted play that Aristotle held the drama to be a nobler form than the epic. " The dramatic poem," said Mr. Henry James some thirty years ago, when he was dealing with Tennyson's 'Queen Mary,' "seems to me of all literary forms the very noblest. . . . More than any other work of literary art, it needs a masterly structure."

Whether nobler or not, the dramatic form has always had a powerful fascination for the novelists, who are forever casting longing eyes on the stage. Mr. James himself has tried it, and Mr. Howells and Mark Twain also. Balzac believed that he was destined to make his fortune in the theater; and one of Thackeray's stories was made over out of a comedy, acted only by amateurs. Charles Reade called himself a dramatist forced to be a novelist by bad laws. Flaubert and the Goncourts, Zola and Daudet wrote original plays, without ever achieving the success which befell their efforts in prose-fiction. And now, in the opening years of the twentieth century, we see Mr. Barrie in London and M. Hervieu in Paris abandoning the novel in which they have triumphed for the far more precarious drama.   Mr. Thomas Hardy also appears to have wearied of the novel and to be seeking relief, if not in real drama, at least in a form borrowed from it, a sort of epic in dialog.   Nor is it without significance that the professional playwrights seem to feel little or no temptation to turn storytellers.   Apparently the dramatic form is the more attractive and the more satisfactory, in spite of its greater difficulty and its greater danger.

Perhaps, indeed, we may discover in this difficulty and danger one reason why the drama is more interesting than prose-fiction.   A true artist cannot but tire of a form that is too facile; and he is ever yearning for a grapple with stubborn resistance.   He delights in technic for its own sake, girding himself joyfully to vanquish its necessities.   He is aware that an art which does not demand a severe apprenticeship for the slow mastery of its secrets will fail to call forth his full strength.   He knows that it is bad for the art and unwholesome for the artist himself, when the conditions are so relaxed that he can take it carelessly.

It was a saying of the old bard of Brittany that "he who will not answer to the rudder must answer to the rocks"; and not a few writers of prose-fiction have made shipwreck because they gave no heed to this warning.   Many a novelist is a sloven in the telling of his tale, beginning it anywhere and ending it somehow, distracting attention on characters of slight importance, huddling his incidents, confusing his narrative, simply because he has never troubled himself with the principles of construction and proportion with which every playwright must needs make himself familiar. Just as the architectural students at the Beaux Arts in Paris are required to develop at the same time the elevation and the ground-plan and the cross-section of the edifice they are designing, so the playwright, while he is working out his plot, must be continually solving problems of exposition and of construction, of contrast and of climax. These are questions with which the ordinary novelist feels no need to concern himself, for the reading public makes no demand on him and there is nothing urging him to attain a high standard. It is worthy of remark that the newspaper reviewers of current fiction very rarely comment on the construction of the novels they are considering.

In other words, the novel is too easy to be wholly satisfactory to an artist in literature. It is a loose form of hybrid ancestry; it may be of any length; and it may be told in any manner, —in letters, as an autobiography or as a narrative. It may win praise by its possession of the mere externals of literature, by sheer style. It may seek to please by description of scenery, or by dissection of motive. It may be empty of action and filled with philosophy. It may be humorously perverse in its license of digression, —as it was in Sterne's hands, for example. It may be all things to all men: it is a very chameleon-weathercock. And it is too varied, too negligent, too lax, to spur its writer to his utmost effort, to that stern wrestle with technic which is a true artist's never-failing tonic.

On the other hand, the drama is a rigid form, limited to the two hours' traffic of the stage. Just as the decorative artist has to fill the space assigned to him and must respect the dispositions of the architect, so the playwright must work his will within the requirements of the theater, turning to advantage the restrictions which he should not evade. He must always appeal to the eye as well as to the ear, never forgetting that the drama, while it is in one aspect a department of literature, in another is a branch of the show-business. He must devise stage-settings at once novel, ingenious and plausible; and he must invent reasons for bringing together naturally the personages of his play in the single place where each of his acts passes. He must set his characters firm on their feet, each speaking for himself and revealing himself as he speaks; for they need to have internal vitality as they cannot be painted from the outside. He must see his creatures as well as hear them; and he must know always what they are doing and how they are looking when they are speaking. He cannot comment on them or explain them, or palliate their misdeeds. He must project them outside of himself; and he cannot be his own lecturer to point out their motives. He must get on without any attempt to point out the morality of his work, which remains implicit altho it ought to be obvious. He must work easily within many bonds, seeming always to be free and unhampered; and he must turn to account these restrictions and find his profit in them, for they are the very qualities which differentiate the drama and make it what it is.

This essential unlikeness of the drama to the novel is so keenly appreciated by every novelist who happens also to be a dramatist, that he is rarely tempted to treat the same theme in both forms, feeling instinctively that it belongs either to the stage or to the library. Often, of course, he writes a novel rather than a play, because he knows that a certain theme, adequate as it may be for a novel, lacks that essential struggle, that naked assertion of the human will, that clash of contending desires, which must be visible in a play if this is to sustain the interest of an audience. Many a tale, pleasing to thousands of readers be-

cause it abounds in brisk adventure, will not lend
itself to successful dramatization because its
many episodes are not related to a single straightforward conflict of forces.

When Mr. Gillette undertook to make a play
out of the Sherlock Holmes stories, which were
not really dramatic, however ingeniously packed
with thrilling surprizes, he seized at once on the
sinister figure of Professor Moriarty, glimpsed
only for a moment in a single tale, and he set this
portentous villain up against his hero, —thereby
displaying his mastery of a major principle of
play-making. Many a novel has seemed vulgarized
on the stage, because the adapter had to wrench
its structure in seeking a struggle strong enough
to sustain the framework of a play. Many a
story has been cheapened pitifully by the theatrical adapter, simply because he was incapable of
seeing in it more than a series of striking scenes
which could be hewn into dialog for rough and
ready representation on the stage, and because he
had seized only his raw material, the bare skeleton
of intrigue, without possessing the skill or the
taste needed to convey across the footlights the
subtle psychology which vitalized the original
tale, or the evanescent atmosphere which
enveloped it in charm. Mr. Bliss Perry phrased
it most felicitously when he asserted that "a
novel is typically as far removed from a play as

a bird is from a fish," and that "the attempt to transform one into the other is apt to result in a sort of flying-fish, a betwixt-and-between thing."

We all know that the ultimate value of certain accepted works of fiction is to be found, not in the story itself or even in the characters, but rather in the interpretative comment with which the novelist has encompassed people and happenings commonplace enough; and we all can see that, when one of these stories is set on the stage, the comment must be stript off, the incidents and the characters standing naked in their triteness. But this betrayal is not to be charged against dramatic form, for all that the dramatization did was to uncover brutally an inherent weakness which the novelist had hoped to hide.

The novelist has privileges denied to the playwright; and, chief among them, of course, is the right to explain his characters, to analize their motives, to set forth every fleeting phase of emotion to which they are subject. Sidney Lanier asserted that the novel was a finer form than the drama because there were subtleties of feeling which Shakspere could not make plain and George Eliot could. Unfortunately for Lanier, his admiration for George Eliot is felt now to be excessive; and few of us are ready to accept Gwendolen Harleth as a more successful attempt at portraiture than any one of half a score of Shakspere's heroines, so convincingly feminine. But there is truth, no doubt, in the contention that the novel is freer, more fluid, more flexible than the play; and that there are themes and subjects unsuited to the stage and wholly within the compass of the story-teller. To say this is but to repeat again that the drama is not prose-fiction and prose-fiction is not the drama,—just as painting is not sculpture and sculpture not painting.

But to emphasize this distinction is not to confess that the drama cannot do at all certain things which the novel does with unconscious ease. Is there no rich variety of self-analysis in 'Macbeth,' one may ask, and in 'Hamlet'? Did any novelist of the seventeenth century lay bare the palpitations of the female heart more delicately than Racine? Did any novelist of the eighteenth century reveal a subtler insight into the hidden recesses of feminine psychology than Marivaux? It may be true enough that, in the nineteenth century, prose-fiction has been more fortunate than the drama and that the novelists have achieved triumphs of insight and of subtlety denied to the dramatists. But who shall say that this immediate inferiority of the play to the novel is inherent in the form itself? Who will deny that it may be merely the defect of the playwrights of our time? Who will assert that a more accomplished dramatist may not come forward in the twentieth century to prove that the drama is a fit instrument for emotional dissection ?

No one has more clearly indicated the limitations of the dramatic medium than Mr. A. B. Walkley, who once declared that the future career of the drama "is likely to be hampered by its inability to tell cultivated and curious people of to-day a tithe of the things they want to know. What the drama can tell, it can tell more emphatically than any other art. The novel, for instance, is but a report; the drama makes you an eye-witness of the thing in the doing. But then there is a whole world of things which cannot be done, of thoughts and moods and subconscious states which cannot be exprest on the stage and which can be exprest in the novel. In earlier ages, which could do with a narrow range of vivid sensations, the drama sufficed; it will not suffice for an age which wants an illimitable range 'of sensations, and, being quick in the uptake, can dispense with vividness." And then the brilliant critic of the London *Times* dwelt on the meagerness of Ibsen's 'Master-Builder' when contrasted with "the extraordinarily complicated texture of subtle thoughts and minute sensations" in Mr. James's 'Wings of the Dove.'

It may as well be confest frankly that, even in the twenty-first century, the playhouse is unlikely to be hospitable to an "extraordinarily complicated texture of subtle thoughts and minute sensations"; but we may ask also if the playhouse will really be very much poorer by this inhospitality. Even tho a small subdivision of the public shall find a keen pleasure in them, there are other things in life than subtle thoughts and minute sensations; there are larger aspects of existence than those we find registered either in the 'Wings of the Dove' or in the 'Master-Builder.' The texture of Mr. James's book may be more complicated than that of Ibsen's play; but this is not entirely because one is a novel and the other a drama. Both works fail in breadth of appeal; they are narrow in their outlook on life, however skilful in craftsmanship they may be, each in its own way; they are devised for the dilettants, for the men of cultivation, and for these mainly; and that way danger lies. Taine dwelt on the disintegration impending when artists tended to appeal to the expert rather than to the public as a whole. "The sculptor," so he declared, "no longer addresses himself to a religious, civic community, but to a group of isolated lovers of the art." In the future as in the past, the appeal of the playwright must be to the main body of his contemporaries, even tho this may be at the risk of not fully satisfying one group or another.

The art of the dramatist is not yet at its richest; but it bristles with obstacles such as a strong man joys in overcoming. In this sharper difficulty is its most obvious advantage over the art of the novelist; and here is its chief attraction for the story-teller, weary of a method almost too easy to be worth while. Here is a reason why one may venture a doubt whether the novel, which has been dominant, not to say domineering, in the second half of the nineteenth century, may not have to face a more acute rivalry of the drama in the first half of the twentieth century. The vogue of the novel is not likely to wane speedily; but its supremacy may be challenged by the drama more swiftly than now seems likely.

(1904.)

THE LITERARY MERIT OF OUR
LATTER-DAY DRAMA

THE LITERARY MERIT OF OUR LATTER-DAY DRAMA

IN trying to present our own opinions upon a question at issue, we can often find an advantage in getting first of all a clear statement of the other side. This must serve as an excuse for here quoting a paragraph (from a British magazine) which chanced to get itself copied in an American newspaper:

The truth is, our dramatists have long since forgotten that the English language is still the medium of the English drama, and that no branch of literary art is worth a word of praise that wantonly divorces itself from literature. The foolish dramatist who was once loquacious concerning what he was pleased to call "the literary drama" condemned his own craft in a single phrase. No doubt, prosperity being essential, the audience of our theaters must share the blame with their favorites. Too idle to listen to exquisite prose or splendid verse, they prefer the quick antics of comedians, and in their ear, as in Mr. Pinero's, "theatrical," has a far more splendid sound than "dramatic." To sum the matter up, that poets have failed upon the stage is no compliment to the professional playwrights, who believe themselves the vessels of an esoteric inspiration. It merely means that literature and the drama travel by different roads, and they will continue to travel by those roads so long as the actor is master of the dramatist, so long as the merits of a drama are judged by the standard of material prosperity. After all, to get your puppets on and off the stage is not the sole end of drama, and modesty might suggest that it is better to fail with Tennyson than to succeed with the gifted author who is at this moment engaged in whitewashing Julia.

Inexpensive in wit as this paragraph is, it serves the purpose of showing us that there are still those who believe the drama of our own time to be a thing of naught. Brief as this quotation is, it is long enough to reveal that the writer of it had the arrogance of ignorance, and that he was expressing what he conceived to be opinions, without taking the trouble to learn anything about the history of the theater or about the principles of the dramatic art.

The full measure of his ignorance it would be a waste of time to point out, but it can be estimated by his two remarks, that it was better to fail with Tennyson than to succeed with Mr. Henry Arthur Jones, and that there is likely to be no change for the better so long as the merits of a drama are judged by "the standard of material prosperity." Taking these assertions in turn, we may note, first, that Tennyson ardently longed to write a play which should please the playgoers of his own time; second, that he desired to be judged by these very standards of material prosperity,—just as Mr. Jones does.

Mr. Jones has more than once succeeded in pleasing the playgoers of his own time, and Tennyson failed to achieve the particular kind of success he was aiming at. His failure may have been due to his lack of the native dramatic faculty; it may have been due to his following of outworn models no longer adjusted to the conditions of the modern theater; but whatever the reason, there is no doubt as to the fact itself. He did not attain the goal he was striving for any more than Browning was able to do so; and it is not for their eulogists now to say that their goal was unworthy. The test of "material prosperity" was the very test by which the poets wisht to be tried, and by this test they both failed—and Mr. Henry Arthur Jones more than once has succeeded. Tennyson and Mr. Jones were aiming at the same target—popular success in the theater. Even if Mr. Jones has not always made a bull's-eye, he has often put his bullet on the target—the very target which Tennyson mist completely, even if his ball happened to make a hit on another.

Tennyson desired to meet the conditions which all the great dramatists have ever been willing to meet. He did not follow their example and study carefully the circumstances of theatrical representation as they had done, nor did he make himself master of the secrets of the dramaturgic art. And this is a chief reason why he was unable to produce any impression upon the drama of his day; while the dramatic poets of the past, the masters whom he respected— Sophocles and Shakspere and Molière—each of them, accepting the formula of the theater as this had been elaborated by his immediate prede- cessors, enlarged this formula, modified it, made it over to suit his own ampler outlook on life, and thus stamped his own individuality upon the drama of succeeding generations.

Shakspere and Molière are accepted by us now as the greatest of dramatic poets; but to their own contemporaries they were known rather as ingenious playwrights up to every trick of the trade, finding their profit in every new device of their fellow-craftsmen, and emerging triumphant from a judgment by "the standard of material prosperity." And by this same standard, un- worthy as it may seem to some, Lope de Vega and Calderon were judged in their own day. Corneille and Racine also, Beaumarchais and Sheridan, Hugo and Augier and Rostand. The standard of material prosperity is not the only test, —indeed, it is not the final test, —but it is the first and the most imperative, because a dramatist who fails to please the play-going public of his own time will never have another chance. There is no known instance of a poet unsuccessful on the stage in his own country and winning recognition in the theater after his death. Posterity never reverses the unfavorable verdict of an author's contemporaries; it has no time to waste on this, for it is too busy reversing the favorable verdicts which seem to it to be in disaccord with the real merits of the case.

It was Mark Twain who pithily summed up a prevailing opinion when he said that " the classics are the books everybody praises—and nobody reads." Let us hope that this is an overstatement and not the exact truth; but whatever the proportion of verity in Mark Twain's saying, there is no doubt that we are running no great risk if we reverse it and say that when they were first produced the classics were books that everybody read—and that nobody praised. Shakspere to-day is the prey of the commentators and of the criticasters, but in his own time Shakspere was the most popular of the Elizabethan playwrights—so popular that his name was tagged to plays he had not written, in order that the public might be tempted to take them into favor. Yet it was years before the discovery was made that this popular playwright was also the greatest poet and the profoundest psychologist of all time. Cervantes lived long enough to be pleased by the widespread enjoyment of his careless masterpiece; but it was a century at least before the first suspicion arose that ' Don Quixote ' was more than a "funny book." Molière was very lucky in filling his theater when his own pieces were performed; but contemporary opinion held that his plays owed their attraction not so much to their literary merit as to the humorous force of his own acting. Molière was acknowledged to be the foremost of comic actors, but only Boileau was sure of his genius as a dramatist; and Boileau's colleagues in the French Academy never recognized Molière's superiority over all his immediate rivals.

The very fact that Molière and Shakspere were pleasing the plain people, that they were able to attract the main body of the unlearned populace, that they sought frankly to be judged by "the standard of material prosperity"—this very fact seems to have prevented their contemporaries from perceiving the literary merit of their plays. Indeed, it is not unfair to suggest that the cultivated critics of the past—like some cultivated critics of our own time—are predisposed to deny literary merit to anything which is broadly popular. They think of literary merit as something upon which they alone are competent to decide, as something to be tried by the touchstones they keep in their studies, under lock and key. The scholarly contemporaries of Shakspere saw that he did not conform to the classic traditions they revered, and they could not guess he was establishing a classic tradition of his own. They were so full of the past that they could not see the present right before their eyes. They mist in Shakspere's work what they had been trained to consider as the chief essential of dramatic art; and they were not acute enough to inquire whether there were not good reasons why he was so attractive to the vulgar mob whom they despised.

To most critics of the drama " literary merit " is something external, something added to the play, something adjusted to the structure. They blame modern playwrights for not putting it in. They take an attitude toward the drama of their own day like that of the New England farmer, when he was asked who had been the architect of his house. " Oh, I built that house myself," was the answer; "but there 's a man coming down from Boston next week to put the architecture on." To this New England farmer, architecture was not in the planning and the proportion and the structure; to him it seemed to mean only some sort of jig-saw fretwork added as an afterthought. To most of those who amuse themselves by writing about the drama, " literary merit " is chiefly a matter of pretty speeches, of phrase-making, of simile and metaphor—in short, of rhetoric.

It seems absurd that at this late day it should be needful to repeat once more that literature is not a matter of rhetoric; that it is not external and detachable, but internal and essential. It has to do with motive and character, with form and philosophy; it is a criticism of life itself, or else it is mere vanity and vexation. If literature is no more than a stringing of flowers of speech, then is 'Lucile' a greater book than 'Robinson Crusoe,' or then is the 'Forest Lovers' a finer book than 'Huckleberry Finn'; then is Pater a better writer than Benjamin Franklin or Abraham Lincoln. Books are not made by style alone. Even lyric poetry is estimated by its fervor and by its sincerity rather than by the dulcet phrases in which the lyrist has voiced his emotion of the moment. If verbal felicity alone is all that the poet needs, if he is to be judged only by the compelling melody of the words he has chosen to set in array, then is Poe the foremost of lyrists. Even the essay, the most narrowly literary of all prose-forms, is valued for its wisdom rather than for its phrasing. The essays of Stevenson, for example, will survive not because of their style alone, polished as that is and unexpectedly happy in its phrasing, but because the man who wrote them, artist as he was in words, had something to say—something which was his own, the result of his own observation of life from his own angle of vision.   Style is the great antiseptic, no doubt; but style cannot bestow life on the still-born.

Not only do such critics as the anonymous writer from whom quotation has been made, persist in thinking of the literary merit of the drama as "exquisite prose" and "splendid verse,"—in other words as an added grace, applied externally,—but they also seem to believe that all plays possessing what they would regard as "literary merit" stand in a class apart.   They are looking for a literary drama which shall be different from the popular drama.   Apparently they expect to be able to recognize a literary play at first sight—and probably by its excess of applied ornament.   And this attitude is quite as absurd as the other.   In no one of the greater periods of the poetic drama have the plays which we now revere as masterpieces differed in form from the mass of the other plays of that epoch.   They were better, no doubt, excelling in power, in elevation, in insight, in skill.   But they bore a striking resemblance in structure and in intent to the host of contemporary plays which we now perceive to be hopelessly inferior to them.

So far as their outward appearance goes the great plays of Sophocles, of Shakspere, and of Molière are closely akin to the plays of their undistinguished contemporaries.   It is in their content that they are immeasurably superior.   They differ in degree only, never in kind. Shakspere early availed himself of the framework of the tragedy-of-blood that Kyd had made popular; and later he borrowed from Beaumont and Fletcher the flexible formula of the dramatic-romance. His genius towered above theirs, but he was content to appropriate their patterns. Molière modeled many of his earlier plays upon the loosely-knit comedy-of-masks of the Italian comedians, and the difference between his work and theirs is not external but internal; it is the difference between adroitness and cleverness on their part, and supreme comic genius on his. Probably it was this apparent similarity of Shakspere's work and Molière's to the uninspired efforts of their competitors which prevented their contemporaries from discovering their preëminence— the preëminence which is so obvious to us now that the plays of their fellow-craftsmen have fallen out of memory.

The blindness of the contemporary critic of Shakspere and of Molière, inexplicable as it may appear nowadays, has its parallel in the blindness of the contemporary critic in regard to 'Don Quixote' and 'Gil Blas,' 'Robinson Crusoe' and the 'Pilgrim's Progress.' He had not the insight to see in these comparatively commonplace narratives the essential truth of the enduring masterpiece. He was seeking an outward and visible sign; he saw nothing unusual, abnormal, eccentric, in these books, nothing novel, nothing that cried aloud for recognition; and so he past by on the other side. These books seemed to him in no wise raised above the common; they were to be enjoyed in some measure, but they evoked no high commendation; and the contemporary critic never suspected that these unpretending volumes, unlike the most of their competitors in public favor, contained the vital spark which alone bestows enduring life. He failed wholly to guess that these books had in them the elements of the universal and the permanent—just as he was unable to perceive that the more obviously literary, rhetorical, academic works he was ready enough to commend highly, lacked these elements and therefore were doomed soon to sink into deserved oblivion.

This is precisely the attitude of many a critic of our own time. He is looking for a literary drama which shall be different in kind from the popular play; and as he fails to find this to-day— as he would have failed to find it in every period of the theater's most splendid achievement—he asserts that the literary drama is nowadays nonexistent. He does not care to inquire into the genuine qualities of the plays that happen to be able to attain "the standard of material prosperity." He is quick to perceive the attempt to be literary in the plays of Mr. Stephen Phillips, because this promising dramatic poet has so far tended rather to construct his decoration than to decorate his construction; and, therefore, the literary merit in Mr. Phillips's acted pieces seems sometimes to be somewhat external, so to speak, or at least more ostentatiously paraded. He is forced to credit 'Quality Street' with a certain literary merit, because Mr. Barrie has published novels which have an undeniable literary flavor.

Considering literary merit as something applied on the outside, too obvious to be mistaken, the critic of this type disdains to give to certain of the plays of Mr. Pinero the discussion they deserve. In the Benefit of the Doubt,' in the 'Second Mrs. Tanqueray,' in 'Iris,' Mr. Pinero has used all his mastery of stage-craft, not for its own sake, but as the instrument of his searching analysis of life as he sees it. All three plays bring out the eternal truth of George Eliot's saying that "Consequences are unpitying." In all three plays the inevitable and inexorable catastrophe is brought about, not by "the long arm of coincidence," but rather by the finger of fate itself. In Iris' more particularly we have put before us the figure of a gentle and kindly creature of compelling personal charm, but weak of will and moving thru life along the line of least resistance—a feminine counterpart of the Tito

Melema etched with such appalling veracity in
'Romola.' And Mr. Pinero has the same sincerity in his portrayal of the gradual disintegration of character under the stress of recurring
temptation, until the woman is driven forth at
last stript of all things that she held desirable,
and bare of the last shred of self-respect. The
play may be unpleasant, but it is profoundly
moral. It is not spoon-meat for babes, but it is
poignant and vital. The picture of human character betrayed by its own weakness is so true, so
transparently sincere, that the spectator, however
quick he may be to discuss the theme, remains
unconscious of the art by which the wonder has
been wrought; he gives scarcely a thought to
the logic of the construction, and to the honesty
with which character is presented — literary
merits both of them, if literature is in fact a criticism of life.

The shrewd remark of M. Jules Lemaître must
ever be borne in mind, — that criticism of our
contemporaries is not criticism, it is only conversation. Yet there is sufficient self-revelation in
the fact that those who have been ready enough
to praise the 'Lady of Lyons,' with its tawdry
rhetoric and its shabby morality, have not seen
the superiority of Mr. Pinero over Lord Lytton
even as a stylist, as a master of English, tense,
nervous, and flexible, adjusting itself to the

thought, never protruding itself on our vision, and yet withstanding verbal criticism when we take time afterward to subject it to that test also.

Just as the Elizabethan critics thought little of Shakspere because he failed to follow in the footsteps of the great Greeks, so some modern critics care naught for the best work of the dramatists of our own time, because this is not cast in the Shaksperian mold. The Elizabethan critics could not know the difference between the theater of Dionysius in Athens and the bare cockpit of the Globe in London; and there are their kin to-day who cannot perceive the difference between the half-roofed playhouse for which Shakspere wrote and the electric-lighted place of amusement to which we are now accustomed. These latter-day critics do not see why the haphazard structure which was good enough for Tudor times is not good enough for us; and they have so little sense of form that they are unaware how the change in the circumstances of performance has forced a more compact presentation of the theme than was necessary in the days of "Eliza and our James."

As Mr. John Morley has pointed out, "the prodigy of such amazing results from such glorious carelessness as Shakspere's has plunged hundreds of men of talent into a carelessness most inglorious." The history of English literature is

strewed with wrecked tragedies, lofty enough in
aspiration, but pitifully lacking in inspiration.
The same tragedies, slovenly as they might be in
structure and empty of dramatic energy, were
cased in the traditional trappings; they were
divided into five acts and they were bedecked with
blank verse; and contemporary critics made haste
to credit them with the literary merit these same
critics do not even look for in 'Iris' and in the
'Second Mrs. Tanqueray,' tragedies, both of
them, of a purifying pathos that Aristotle would
have understood. In fact, there would be no
great difficulty in showing how near Aristotle
came to an explicit assertion that in the drama
"literary merit" is almost a by-product—valuable,
no doubt, like many another by-product, but not
the chief thing to be sought.

Mr. Pinero has discust Robert Louis Stevenson
as a dramatist, and his lecture contained passages
which every man of letters should ponder. He
showed that Stevenson had in him the true
dramatic stuff, but that he refused to serve the
severe apprenticeship to play-making that he
gladly gave to novel-writing. Mr. Pinero made
plain the further fact that Stevenson, who was
ever a sedulous ape of the masters he admired,
had here set himself a bad pattern to copy. This
was not the loose and rambling Elizabethan model
which had led Tennyson and Browning astray;

it was the model of the cheap melodrama of the early years of the nineteenth century. "Stevenson with all his genius failed to realize that the art of drama is not stationary, but progressive," said Mr. Pinero. "By this I do not mean that it is always improving; what I do mean is that its conditions are always changing and that every dramatist whose ambition it is to produce live plays is absolutely bound to study carefully . . . the conditions that hold good for its own age and generation."

This is what every great dramatist has done; it is what Shakspere did and Molière also; it is what Stevenson did not care to do, because he did not understand the necessity of it. He did not borrow the formula of the most successful of the plays which chanced to be pleasing the public jus_ then. If he had done this, he could have put into this formula all the fine writing he so much enjoyed; he might have given to his plays the utmost polish of style. Instead of trying to write dramas externally like those popular in the theater of his own time, and making them internally whatsoever he chose, he went back half a century and tried to revive a poor formula already defunct. The game was lost before the cards were dealt. He had refused to consider the conditions of the problem he was handling—"the problem of how to tell a dramatic story truly, convincingly, and effectively, on the modern stage"; as Mr. Pinero described it, "the problem of disclosing the workings of the human heart by methods which shall not destroy the illusion which a modern audience expects to enjoy in the modern theater."

Stevenson was here making the mistake which so many men of letters make when they turn to the theater. He was going upon the theory that the drama is made literary, not from within, by observation and imagination and sincerity, but from without, by the application of fine speeches. His speeches were fine, no doubt, even tho they were not in keeping with that special kind of play when it had been alive. But as it happened, that kind of play was dead and gone, and no injection of oratory would bring it to life again. And here the Scotch story-teller failed to profit by the example of the French poet whose romances he had so sympathetically studied. Hugo had also a gift for oratory and a talent for fine speeches; but when he yearned for theatrical success he went to the most popular playhouses where the plain people gathered, and he adopted as his own the formula of play-making which was proving its value in these boulevard theaters. This was not in itself much better than the formula Stevenson borrowed and did not trouble to understand—indeed, the two are not unlike. But Hugo had made his choice half a century before Stevenson; and when he made it he was taking possession of the very latest fashion.

Hugo's formula is now fallen out of mode, yet his plays have accomplished their threescore years and ten. It was Hugo who declared that there are three classes of theater-goers whom the play-wright must please: the crowd that demands action, the women who wish for emotion, and the thinkers who seek for character. And it was Hugo's early rival as a play-maker, the elder Dumas, who asserted that the only rules he knew for success upon the stage were to make the first act clear, the last act short, and all the acts interesting. A dramatist who shall accept the formula which has been found satisfactory by his immediate contemporaries, and who shall succeed in making all the acts of his play interesting alike to the crowd, to the women, and to the thinkers, will be very likely to achieve literary merit without striving for it specifically.

For we cannot repeat too often that in the drama "literary merit" is a by-product,—as it is in oratory also. And we cannot assert too emphatically that the drama has an independent existence—that it does not lie wholly within the domain of literature. "The art of the drama," so M. Emile Faguet has assured us, "touches all the other arts and includes them." The drama is not intended primarily to be read in the study; it is devised to be performed on the stage by actors before spectators. It has a right, therefore, to avail itself of the aid of all other arts and to enlist them all in its service. This is one of the reasons why those who have studied the secrets of this art are inclined to esteem it as the noblest and most powerful of them all. As M. Faguet has declared, with that sympathetic understanding of the essential principles of the drama which is common enough in France and only too rare elsewhere—"it is not contradictory to the definition of dramatic art that it can synthesize in space like painting, that it can synthesize in time like poetry, that it can synthesize outside of time and space like music, that it can unite all the arts without forcing them to interfere the one with the other, and, therefore, without taking from any one aught of its force or aught of its dignity; that it can unite them all in a vast, powerful, and harmonious synthesis embracing the whole of life and the whole of art."

(1903.)

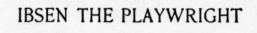

IBSEN THE PLAYWRIGHT

IBSEN THE PLAYWRIGHT

I

ONE indisputable service has Ibsen rendered to the drama: he has revealed again that it may be an incomparable instrument in the hands of a poet-philosopher who wishes to make people think, to awaken them from an ethical lethargy, to shock them into asking questions for which the complacent morality of the moment can provide no adequate answer. In the final decades of the nineteenth century,— when the novel was despotic in its overwhelming triumph over all the other forms of literary expression, and when arrogant writers of fiction like Edmond de Goncourt did not hesitate to declare that the drama was outworn at last, that it was unfitted to convey the ideas interesting to the modern world, and that it had fallen to be no more than a toy to amuse the idle after dinner, —Ibsen brought forth a succession of social dramas as tho to prove that the playhouse of our own time could supply a platform whereon a man might free his soul and boldly deliver his message, if only he had first mastered the special conditions of the playwright's art. Of course, Ibsen has solved none of the problems he has propounded; nor was it his business as a dramatist to provide solutions of the strange enigmas of life, but rather to force us to exert ourselves to find each of us the best answer we could.

No one who has followed the history of the theater for the past quarter of a century can fail to acknowledge that these social plays of Ibsen have exerted a direct, an immediate and a powerful influence on the development of the contemporary drama. It is easy to dislike them; indeed, it is not hard even to detest them; but it is impossible to deny that they have been a stimulus to the dramatists of every modern language—and not least to playwrights of various nationalities wholly out of sympathy with Ibsen's own philosophy. The fascination of these social dramas may be charmless, as Mr. Henry James once asserted; but there is no gainsaying the fascination itself. As M. Maeterlinck has declared, Ibsen is "perhaps the only writer for the stage who has caught sight of and set in motion, a new, tho still disagreeable, poetry, which he has succeeded in investing with a kind of savage, gloomy beauty"; and M. Maeterlinck then questions whether this beauty is not too savage and too gloomy to become general or definitive. But, none the less, it is at least beauty, a quality long banished from the stage, when Ibsen showed how it might be made to bloom there again.

Nor is there any dispute as to the variety and the veracity of the characters that people these studies from life. Indeed, as Mr. Archer once pointed out, "habitually and instinctively men pay to Ibsen the compliment (so often paid to Shakspere) of discussing certain of his female characters as tho they were real women, living lives apart from the poet's creative intelligence." And in yet another way is Ibsen treated like Shakspere, in that there is superabundant discussion not only of his characters, male and female, but also of his moral aim, of his sociological intention, of his philosophy of life, while very little attention is paid to his dramaturgic craftsmanship, to his command of structural beauty, to his surpassing skill in the difficult art of the play-maker. Yet Shakspere and Ibsen are professional playwrights, both of them, each making plays adjusted exactly to the conditions of the theater of his own time; and if the author of 'Othello' can prove himself (when the spirit moves him) to be a master-technician, so also can the author of 'Ghosts.'

There is ample recognition of Ibsen as the ardent reformer seeking to blow away the mists of

sentimentality, and of Ibsen, the symbolist, suggesting dimly a host of things unseen and
strangely beautiful; but there is little consideration of Ibsen's solid workmanship, of his sure
knowledge of all the secrets of the stage, of his
marvelous dexterity of exposition, construction
and climax. No doubt, it is as a poet, in the
largest meaning of the word, that Ibsen is most
interesting; but he is a playwright also,—indeed,
he is a playwright, first and foremost; and in
that aspect also he is unfailingly interesting. For
those who insist that a poet must be a philosopher, Ibsen is to be ranked with Browning as af-
fording endless themes for debate; but for those
who demand that a dramatic poet shall be a playwright, Ibsen is a rival of Scribe and of the
younger Dumas and of all the school of accomplished craftsmen in France who have made Paris
the capital of the dramatic art. Ibsen's skill as a
playwright is so consummate that his art is never
obtruded. In fact, it was so adroitly hidden that
when he first loomed on the horizon, careless
theatrical critics were tempted rather to deny its
existence. He is such a master of all the tricks
of the trade that he can improve upon them or do
without them, as occasion serves; and perhaps
it is only those thoroly familiar with the practises
of the accomplished French playwrights of the
nineteenth century who perceive clearly the su-

periority of Ibsen in the mere mechanism of the dramaturgical art.

II

ALTHO it is possible to consider his stage-technic apart from his teaching, it needs to be noted at the outset that Ibsen the playwright owes a large portion of his power and effectiveness to Ibsen the poet-philosopher. As it happens, the doctrine of individual responsibility, which is the core of Ibsen's code, is a doctrine most helpful to the dramatist. The drama, indeed, differentiates itself from all other literary forms in that it must deal with a struggle, with a clash of contending desires, with the naked assertion of the human will. This is the mainspring of that action without which a drama is a thing of naught; and perhaps the most obvious backbone for a play is the tense contest of two human beings, each knowing clearly what he wants and each straining to attain it, at whatever cost to his adversary, to all others, and even to himself. Rivals fighting to the death, a hero at war with the world, a single soul striving to wrench itself free from the fell clutch of fate,— such is the stuff out of which the serious drama must be compounded.

Now, as it happens, no philosopher has ever

reiterated more often than Ibsen his abhorrence of smug and complacent compromise, his belief in the unimpeded independence of the individual, his conviction that every creature here below owes it as a duty to himself to live his own life in his own way. Just as *Brand* stiffens himself once more and makes the implacable declaration:

> Beggar or rich,—with all my soul
> I *will;* and that one thing 's the whole !

So *Dr. Stockman* announces his discovery that "the strongest man upon earth is he who stands most alone"; and in every play we find characters animated by this unhesitating determination and this unfaltering energy. Even Ibsen's women, so subtly feminine in so many ways, are forever revealing themselves virile in their self-assertion, in their claim to self-ownership. His plays move us strangely in the performance, they grip at the outset and firmly hold us to the relentless end, because his dramaturgic skill is exerted upon themes essentially dramatic in that they deal with this stark exhibition of the human will and with the bitter struggle that must ensue when the human will is in revolt against the course of nature or against the social bond.

When the poet-philosopher has suggested to the playwright one of these essentially dramatic themes, Ibsen handles it with a directness which intensifies its force and which is in itself evidence of his poetic power. As Professor Butcher has pointed out, "we are perhaps inclined to rate too low the genius which is displayed in the general structure of an artistic work; we set it down merely as the hard-won result of labor, and we find inspiration only in isolated splendors, in the lightning-flash of passion, in the revealing power of poetic imagery." In these last gifts Ibsen may seem to many, if not deficient, at least, less abundant than some other dramatic poets; but he can attain "the supreme result which Greek thought and imagination achieve by their harmonious coöperation"; he can present "the organic union of parts." He has the sense of form which we feel to be the final guerdon of Greek endeavor.

A play of Ibsen's is always compact and symmetrical. It has a beginning, a middle, and an end; it never straggles, but ever moves straightforward to its conclusion. It has unity; and often it conforms even to the pseudo-unities proclaimed by the superingenious critics of the Italian renascence. Sometimes a play of Ibsen's has another likeness to a tragedy of the Greeks, in that it presents in action before the assembled spectators only the culminating scenes of the story. 'Ghosts' recalls 'Œdipus the King,' not only in the horror at the heart of it and the poignancy of the emotion it evokes, but also in its being a fifth act only, the culmination of a long and complex concatenation of events, which took place before the point at which Sophocles and Ibsen saw fit to begin their plays. In the Greek tragedy, as in the Scandinavian social drama, the poet has chosen to deal with the result of the action, rather than with the visible struggle itself; it is not the present doings of the characters, but their past deeds, which determine their fate.

Altho no other play of Ibsen's attains the extraordinary compactness and swiftness of 'Ghosts,' several of them approach closely to this standard, the 'Master-Builder,' for example, 'Little Eyolf' and more especially 'Rosmersholm,'—in which the author did not display on the stage itself more than a half of the strong series of situations he had devised to sustain the interest of the spectator and to elucidate his underlying thesis. But Ibsen does not hold himself restricted to any one formula; and sometimes he prefers, as in the 'Enemy of the People,' to let the whole story unroll itself before the audience. Only slowly did Ibsen come to a mastery of his own methods; and he had begun, in the 'League of Youth' and in the 'Pillars of Society' by doing what every great dramatist had done before him, —by accepting the form worked out by his im-

mediate predecessors and adjusted to the actual
theater of his own time. Just as Shakspere followed the patterns set by Kyd and Marlowe, by
Lyly and Greene, just as Molière copied the model
ready to his hand in the Italian comedy-of-masks,
so Ibsen began by assimilating the formulas
which had approved themselves in France, the
land where the drama was flourishing most luxuriantly in the middle of the nineteenth century,
formulas devised by Scribe and only a little modified by Augier and the younger Dumas.

III

FOR threescore years, at least, Scribe was the
salient figure in the French theater; and his influence endured more than twoscore years after
his death. He can be considered from discordant
standpoints; to the men of letters Scribe seems
wholly unimportant, since his merits were in great
measure outside of literature; to the men of the
theater Scribe is a personality of abiding interest,
since he put his mark on the drama of his own
day in almost every one of its departments. In
the course of his active career as a playwright he
made over farce, first of all, then the comedy-of-
intrigue, and finally the comedy-of-manners; he
tried his hand at the historical play; and he was
the chief librettist of the leading French com-

posers of opera, both grand and comic. He might lack style; he might be barren of poetry; he might be void of philosophy; his psychology might be pitifully inadequate; his outlook on life might be petty;—but he was pastmaster of the theater, and from him were hidden none of the secrets of that special art.

It was in Scribe's hands that there was worked out the formula of the "well-made play,—" *la pièce bien faite*,—in which the exposition was leisurely and careful, in which the interest of expectancy was aroused early and sustained to the end, in which the vital scenes of the essential struggle,—the *scènes à faire*,—were shown on the stage at the very moment of the story when they would be most effective, and in which a logical conclusion dimly foreseen, but ardently desired, was happily brought about by devices of unexpected ingenuity. In perfecting the formula of the "well-made play" Scribe may have taken hints from Beaumarchais, especially from the final act of the 'Marriage of Figaro'; and he had found his profit also in a study of the methods of the melodrama, which had been elaborated in the theaters of the Parisian boulevards at the beginning of the nineteenth century, and which had been imitated already by Hugo and the elder Dumas. At its best, the "well-made play" was an amusing piece of mechanism, a clockwork toy which had a mere semblance of life, but which did precisely what its maker had constructed it to do.

The piece put together according to this formula was sufficient to itself, with its wheels within wheels; and its maker had no need of style or of poetry, of psychology or of philosophy. So long as the playwright was content to be a playwright only and did not aspire to be a dramatist with his own views of life, the formula was satisfactory enough; but when the younger Dumas and Augier came on the stage they wanted to put a broader humanity into their plays, and they could make room for this only by simplifying the machinery. Yet, while they were delivering each his own message, they accepted the model of the "well-made play"; and it is to this that we may ascribe the artificiality we begin to discern even in such masterpieces of dramaturgic craftsmanship as the 'Gendre de M. Poirier' and the 'Demi-monde.'

Upon Ibsen also the influence of Scribe is as obvious as it is upon Augier and Dumas *fils*. The earliest of his social dramas, the 'League of Youth' and the 'Pillars of Society' are composed according to the formula of the "well-made play," with its leisurely exposition, its intricate complications of recoiling intrigue, its ingeniously contrived conclusion. If we compare the

'League of Youth' with Scribe's 'Bertrand et Raton,' or with Sardou's 'Rabagas'; if we compare the 'Pillars of Society' with Dumas's 'Étrangère,' or Augier's 'Effrontés' we cannot fail to find a striking similarity of structure. Set even 'A Doll's House' by the side of any one of a dozen contemporary French comedies, and it is easy to understand why Sarcey declared that play to be Parisian in its construction, — up to the moment of *Nora's* revolt and self-assertion, so contrary to the social instinct of the French. And this explains also why it was that Ibsen, as Herr Lindau has told us, made little or no impression on the German dramatists until after the appearance of 'Ghosts,' altho the preceding plays had been acted frequently in the German theaters. The scenes of these early plays are laid in Norway, it is true, and the characters are all Norwegian, and altho it is easy enough for us, to-day, with our knowledge of what Ibsen has become, to find in them the personal equation of the author, still he was then frankly continuing the French tradition of stage-craft, with a willing acceptance of the formula of the "well-made play" and with no effort after novelty in his dramaturgic method. Not until he brought forth the 'Ghosts' is there any overt assertion of his stalwart and aggressive personality.

In the beginning Ibsen was no innovator. So

far at least as its external form is concerned, the kind of play he proffered at first was very much what actors and audiences alike had been accustomed to,—a kind of play perfectly adjusted to the existing customs of the stage. What he did was to take over the theater as a going concern, holding himself free to modify the accepted formula only after he had mastered it satisfactorily. Considering Ibsen's inexperience as a writer of prose-plays dealing with contemporary life, the 'League of Youth' is really very remarkable as a first attempt. Indeed, its defects are those of its models; and it errs chiefly in its excess of ingenuity and in the manufactured symmetry of the contrivance whereby the tables are turned on *Stensgard*, and whereby he loses all three of the women he has approached.

As Lowell has said: "It is of less consequence where a man buys his tools than what use he makes of them"; but it so happened that Ibsen acquired his stage-craft in the place where it is most easily attained, in the place where Shakspere and Molière had acquired it,—in the theater itself. In 1851, when he was only twenty-three, he had been appointed "theater-poet" to the newly opened playhouse in Bergen; and after five years there he had gone to Christiania to be director of a new theater, where he was to remain yet another five years. In this decade of his impressionable and plastic youth Ibsen had taken part in the production of several score plays, some of them his own, others also original in his native tongue by Holberg and Öhlenschläger, and many more translated from Scribe, from Scribe's collaborators and from Scribe's contemporaries. In his vacation travels, to Copenhagen and to Dresden, he had opportunity to observe a wider variety of plays; but even in these larger cities the influence of Scribe was dominant, as it was all over the civilized world in the mid-years of the century.

As Fenimore Cooper, when he determined to tell the fresh story of the backwoods and the prairies, found a pattern ready to his hand in the Waverley novels, so Ibsen availed himself of the "well-made play" of Scribe when he wrote the 'League of Youth,' which is his earliest piece in prose presenting contemporary life and character in Norway. There is obvious significance in the fact that of all Ibsen's dramas, those which have won widest popularity in the theater itself are those which most frankly accept the Gallic framework,—the 'Pillars of Society,' the 'Doll's House,' and 'Hedda Gabler.' Yet it is significant, also, that even in the least individual of Ibsen's earlier pieces, the action is expressive of character; and we cannot fail to see that Ibsen's personages control the plot; whereas, in the dramas of Scribe, the situations may be said almost to create the characters, which, indeed, exist only for the purposes of that particular story.

<h2 style="text-align:center">IV</h2>

In spite of Ibsen's ten years of apprenticeship in two theaters, in daily contact with the practical business of the stage, it was not with prose-dramas of contemporary life that he first came forward as a dramatist. In fact, his juvenile 'Katilina' (1850) was written when he was but just of age, before he was attached to the theater professionally, before he had read any dramatists except Holberg and Öhlenschläger, and before he had had the chance to see much real acting on the stage itself. It was while he was engaged in producing the plays of others that he brought out also his own 'Mistress Inger at Ostraat' (1855), and the 'Vikings at Helgeland' (1858), both of them actable and often acted. They are romanticist in temper, suggesting now Schiller and now Hugo.

'Mistress Inger' is a historical melodrama, with a gloomy castle, spectral pictures and secret passages, with shifting conspiracies, constant mystery-mongering and contorted characters. The inexpert playwright uses soliloquy not merely to unveil the soul of the speaker (its eternally legitimate use), but also to convey information to the audience as to the facts of the intrigue (an outworn expedient Ibsen never condescended to use in the later social dramas). The plot of 'Mistress Inger' is not veracious or convincing or even plausible; and the play lacks the broad simplicity of story to be found in the later 'Vikings,' a saga-like drama, a tale of blood and fate, which recalls Wagnerian opera in its primitive massiveness, in the vigor of its legend, in its tragic pathos, and in its full-blooded characters larger than life and yet pitifully human. Power again there is in a third drama dealing with the historic past of Norway, the 'Pretenders' (1864), which has a savage nobility of spirit. It is true that the masterful figure of *Bishop Nicholas* is enigmatic enough to have stalked out of one of Hugo's lyrical melodramas, but to counterbalance this there is a pithy wisdom in the talk of the *Skald* which one would seek in vain in the French romanticist drama.

Nowadays many of us are inclined to regard the historical drama as a bastard form and to agree with Maeterlinck in dismissing even the most meritorious attempts as "artificial poems that arise from the impossible marriage of past and present." Already between the 'Vikings' and the 'Pretenders' had Ibsen undertaken a play dealing with contemporary social usages. 'Love's Comedy' (1862) made its way on the stage; and it has found an English translator. But in this rendering it reveals itself as an attempt to commingle romance and satire; it appears to us as hopelessly unfunny; and there is an artistic inconsistency between a stern realism seeking to handle actual life with rigorous tensity and a soaring idealism which keeps obtruding itself.

'Love's Comedy' is in verse, irregular and rimed, well-nigh impossible to render satisfactorily into another tongue. Ibsen never again undertook to use rime or even meter in handling the manners of his own time. "I cannot believe that meter will be employed to any considerable extent in the drama of the near future, for the poetic intentions of the future cannot be reconciled with it," so Ibsen declared in 1883, thus passing judgment on 'Love's Comedy.' And he added that he had written scarcely any verse for years but "had exclusively cultivated the incomparably more difficult art of writing in the even, beautiful idiom of real life."

It was in 1857 that Björnson had put forth 'Synnöve Solbakken,' a mere novelet, it is true, but still the firstling of a native Norwegian literature, reproducing the very accent of the soil; and here we have once more an example of the way in which the novel is now continually affecting the development of the drama, as the play has in the past influenced the evolution of prose-fiction. For more than ten years Ibsen failed to see how much it would profit him to follow Björnson's lead. Between 'Love's Comedy' and the 'League of Youth' he put forth his two great dramatic poems, 'Brand' (1866) and 'Peer Gynt' (1867); and even after the 'League of Youth' (1869) had opened the series of modern social dramas, he published 'Emperor and Galilean' (1873) before resuming his incisive study of the life that lay around him.

The career of Julian the Apostate is sketched in what must be termed a chronicle-play, in two parts and in ten acts, a broadly brushed panorama of antique life, displaying Ibsen's abundant invention, his ability to handle boldly a large theme, his gift of putting characters erect on their feet with a few swift strokes. Altho 'Emperor and Galilean,' like 'Brand' and like 'Peer Gynt' was intended for the closet only, and not for the stage itself, it proves its author to be a true dramatist, centering the interest of his story on an essential struggle and keeping in view always the pictorial aspects of his action.

In this chronicle-play, as in his two greater dramatic poems, Ibsen reveals his perfect understanding of the practical necessities of the play-house, even tho he did not choose always to conform to them. Then he turned his back on antiquity and faced the present in the series of prose-plays by which he is most widely known to actual playgoers. He found his characters and his themes in modern life and in his native land; and the social dramas followed one another in steady succession, — 'Pillars of Society' (1877), 'A Doll's House' (1879), 'Ghosts' (1881), 'An Enemy of the People' (1882), the 'Wild Duck' (1884), 'Rosmersholm' (1886), the 'Lady from the Sea' (1888), 'Hedda Gabler' (1890), the 'Master-Builder' (1892), 'Little Eyolf' (1894), 'John Gabriel Borkman' (1896) and 'When We Dead Awaken' (1899).

As we look down this list, we see that it is perhaps unfair to class all the later plays as social dramas. Some of them, more especially the latest of them all, 'When We Dead Awaken,' seem to be symbolical rather than social, allegorical in intent even if they remain realistic in treatment. Brandes long ago declared that Ibsen had had a Pegasus killed under him; but when we consider the 'Lady from the Sea' and 'When We Dead Awaken' and perhaps one or two other of their later companions, we may well believe that the winged steed was not actually slain. Wounded it may have been, only to recover its strength again and to proffer its back once more for the poet to bestride.

V

THESE more poetic of Ibsen's plays in prose seem at times almost surcharged with a meaning which is nevertheless often so mockingly intangible and evasive, that we dare to wonder at last whether the secret they persist in hiding in this tantalizing fashion would really reward our efforts to grasp it; and we find comfort in Lowell's apt saying that "to be misty is not to be mystic." Ibsen is mystic, no doubt, but on occasion he can be misty also. And not only the plays that are merely misty but even those that are truly mystic, are less likely than the plainer-spoken social dramas to hold our attention in the theater itself, where the appeal is to the assembled multitude, and where all things need to be clearly defined so that the spectators can follow understandingly every phase of the changing action.

In the most of his social dramas Ibsen makes his meaning transparentlyclear; and there is never any undue strain on the attention of the average playgoer. Especially is he a master of the difficult art of exposition. It is the plain duty of the playwright to acquaint the audience with the antecedent circumstances upon which the plot is based, —to inform the spectators fully as to that part of the story which has gone before and which is not to be displayed in action on the stage, —to explain the relation of the several characters to each other,—and to arouse interest in what is about to happen. Scribe, than whom no one ever had a wider knowledge of the necessities of the theater, held the exposition to be so important that he often sacrificed to it the whole of his first act, introducing his characters one by one, setting forth clearly what had happened before the play, and sometimes postponing the actual beginning of the action to the end of the first act, if not to the earlier scenes of the second. Scribe seems to have believed that it did not matter much how dull the first act might be, since the spectators had paid their money and would not abandon hope until they had seen at least the second act, in which he sought always to grip their interest.

In the 'League of Youth,' the earliest of his social dramas, Ibsen follows in Scribe's footsteps; and the first act is little more than a preparatory prolog. In this play the whole story is set forth in action in the play itself; but in the following dramas, 'Pillars of Society' and 'A Doll's House' Ibsen reveals his tendency to deal with the results of deeds which took place before he begins the play itself. In other words, he suppresses his prolog, preferring to plunge at once into his action; and this forces him to modify Scribe's leisurely method. He does not mass his explanations all in the earlier scenes; he scatters them

thruout the first act, and sometimes he even post-
pones them to the later acts. But he is careful
to supply information before it is needed, adroitly
letting out in the first scene what is required for
the understanding of the second scene, and artfully revealing in the second scene what must be
known before the third scene can be appreciated.

This method is less simple than Scribe's; it is
not only more difficult, it may be dangerous;
but when it is managed successfully it lends to
the drama a swift directness delightful to all who
relish a mastery of form. In 'Ghosts,' for example, the play which is acted before us is little
more than a long fifth act, in three tense scenes;
and the knowledge of what had happened in the
past is ingeniously communicated to the audience
at the very moment when the information is felt
to be most significant. But in 'Rosmersholm,'
strong as the drama is and fine as its technic is,
Ibsen's method seems to be at fault in that we
learn too late what it would have interested us
greatly to know earlier. It is only at the end
almost that we are allowed to perceive what
were *Rebecca West's* real intentions in coming to
Rosmersholm and how the influence of the house
itself has transformed her. When the curtain
rises she is presented to us already a changed
woman; and we are at a loss to understand her
motives for the evil deeds she has wrought, until

we are told at last that she once was far different from what she now is. Here Ibsen loses more than he gains by abandoning the simpler method of massing his exposition in the earlier scenes of the play. Anything which confuses the spectator, which leaves him in doubt, which keeps him guessing, is contrary to Spencer's principle of "economy of attention," as important in the other arts as it is in rhetoric.

Altho he is ever seeking to awaken curiosity, to arouse the interest of expectancy, and to excite in the spectators a desire to see the thing through, Ibsen refrains from any mere mystery-mongering for its own sake. He wishes his audience to give attention not so much to the bare happenings of his story, however startling they may be in themselves, as to the effect which these happenings are certain to have on the characters. He is abundant in inventive ingenuity and in devising effective situations; and the complications of the plot of the 'Pillars of Society' would probably have hugely pleased Scribe. But he has also the larger imagination which can people situation with character and which can make situation significant as an opportunity for character to express itself. Ingenious as he is in plot-building, with him character always dominates situation. To Ibsen character is destiny, and the persons of his plays seem to have created, by their own natural proceeding, the predicaments in which they are immeshed.

Ibsen is particularly happy in the subordinate devices by which he reveals character,—for example, *Maia's* taking off the green shade when the *Master-Builder* enters the room. And another device, that of the catchword, which he took over from Scribe and the younger Dumas, and which, even in his hands, remains a mere trick in the early 'League of Youth,' is so delicately utilized in certain of the later plays—witness, the "vine-leaves in his hair" of 'Hedda Gabler' and the "white horses" in 'Rosmersholm'—that these recurrent phrases are transformed into a prose equivalent of Wagner's leading-motives. So, too, Ibsen does without the *raisonneur* of Dumas and Augier, that condensation of the Greek chorus into a single person, who is only the mouthpiece of the author himself and who exists chiefly to point the moral, even tho he may sometimes also adorn the tale. Ibsen so handles his story that it points its own moral; his theme is so powerfully presented in action that it speaks for itself.

It must also be noted that Ibsen, like all born playwrights, like Scribe and Dumas and Augier, like Sophocles and Shakspere and Molière, is well aware of the double aspect of the theater, in that the stage can rise to the loftiest heights of philosophic poetry and that it can fall also to the lowest depths of the show-business. An audience has ears, but the spectators who compose it have eyes also; and the born playwright never fails to provide the picturesqueness and the visible movement which satisfy the senses, whatever may be the more serious appeal to the mind. In the modern theater the stage is withdrawn behind a picture-frame; and it is the duty of the dramatist to satisfy our demand for a stage-setting pictorially adequate. The sets of Ibsen's plays have evidently been sharply visualized by him; they are elaborately described; and they lend themselves effectively to the art of the scene-painter. Sometimes they are beautiful in themselves, novel and suggestive; always are they characteristic of the persons and of the underlying idea of the play.

VI

WHEN we examine carefully the earlier of his social dramas we discover Ibsen to be a playwright of surpassing technical dexterity, whose work is sustained and stiffened and made more valuable and more vital by the coöperation of the philosopher that Ibsen also is, a philosopher who is a poet as well and who helps the playwright to find the stuff he handles, the raw material of his art, in the naked human soul, in its doubts and its perplexities, in its blind gropings and in its ineffectual strivings. But in considering the later plays we are forced to wonder whether the philosopher has not gained the upper hand and reduced the playwright to slavery.

It was of Ibsen, no doubt, that M. Maeterlinck was thinking when he asserted that " the first thing which strikes us in the drama of the day is the decay, one might almost say, the creeping paralysis, of external action. Next, we note a very pronounced desire to penetrate deeper into human consciousness, and to place moral problems on a high pedestal." And there is no denying that Ibsen's interest in moral problems has grown steadily in intensity, and that he has sought to penetrate deeper and deeper into human consciousness. His latest play, 'When We Dead Awaken,' altho adjusted to the conditions of the modern theater and altho perfectly actable, seems to be intended rather more for the reader than for the spectator. Essentially dramatic as it is, its theatric realization is less satisfactory—as tho Ibsen was chafing against the restraints of the actual theater, restraints which are an integral element of its power as a form of expression.

In the same suggestive essay, M. Maeterlinck remarked on the steady decline of the taste for bald theatrical anecdotes, —the taste which Scribe and Sardou were content to gratify; and he declared that "mere adventures fail to interest us because they no longer correspond to a living and actual reality." And yet no one has more sharply proclaimed the sovran law of the stage than the Belgian critic-poet; no one has more sympathetically asserted that "its essential demand will always be *action*. With the rise of the curtain, the high intellectual desire within us undergoes transformation; and in place of the thinker, psychologist, mystic, or moralist, there stands the mere instinctive spectator, the man electrified negatively by the crowd, the man whose one desire is to see something happen." In his later and more poetic plays Ibsen seems to be appealing more especially to the mystic and the moralist; whereas in the earlier social dramas he was able to grip the attention of the mere instinctive spectator, while also satisfying the unexprest desires of the thinker.

The sheer symbolism of the poet-philosopher is powerfully suggestive, and these later plays have an interest of their own, no doubt; but it is in the earlier social dramas that Ibsen most clearly reveals his dramaturgic genius, —in the ' Pillars of Society,' and the ' Doll's House,' in ' Ghosts ' and in ' Hedda Gabler.' Dennery might envy the ingenuity with which *Consul Bernick* is tempted to insist on the fatal order that seems for a season to be the death-sentence of his own son; and Sardou would appreciate the irony of *Nora's* frantic dance at the very moment when she was tortured by deadly fear. But these theatric devices, in Dennery's hands or in Sardou's, would have existed for their own sake solely; but in Ibsen's, effective as they are, they have a deeper significance. He is able to avail himself of the complicated machinery of the " well-made play," to flash a piercing light into the darker recesses of human nature. However clever he may be in his handling of these scenes, his cleverness is a means only; it is not an end in itself. He never gives over " his habit of dealing essentially with the individual caught in the fact,"—to borrow an apt phrase from Mr. Henry James. The mechanism may be almost as elaborate as it is in a play of Scribe's, wherein there is ultimately nothing but ingenuity of invention and adroitness of construction; but it is never allowed to crush or to keep out human nature.

Consul Bernick is one of Ibsen's most veracious characters, with his cloaking morality, his unconscious egotism, and his unfaltering selfishness, disclosed so naïvely and so naturally. Less boldly drawn but not the less truthful is *Helmer*, that inexpugnable prig, with his shallow selfishness, his complacent conceit, and his morality for external use only. Ibsen is never happier, and never is his scalpel more skilful, than when he is laying bare the hollowness of shams like these. Never is his touch more delicate or more caressing than when he is delineating a character like *Bernick's* sister *Martha*, with her tender devotion and her self-effacing simplicity. Not even *Helmer's* wife, *Nora*, is more truthfully conceived. *Nora* is veraciously feminine in never fathoming *Dr. Rank's* love for her, or at least in her refusal to formulate it, content to take his friendship and ask herself no questions. Truly womanly again is her attitude when he speaks out at last and thrusts upon her the knowledge of his passion,—her shrinking withdrawal, her instant ordering in of the lights, and her firm refusal then, in her hour of need, to profit by the affection he has just declared.

It must be regretted that Ibsen does not dismiss either *Nora* or *Bernick* with the final fidelity that might have been expected. *Bernick's* unexpected proclamation of his change of heart, so contrary to his habits, is a little too like one of those fantastic wrenchings of veracity of which Dickens was so often guilty in the finishing chapters of his stories. Character is never made over in the twinkling of an eye; and this is why the end of the 'Doll's House' seems unconvincing. *Nora*, the morally irresponsible, is suddenly endowed

with clearness of vision and directness of speech.
The squirrel who munches macaroons, the song-
bird who is happy in her cage, all at once becomes a raging lioness.   And this is not so much
an awakening or a revelation, as it is a transformation; and the *Nora* of the final scenes of the
final act is not the *Nora* of the beginning of the
play.   The swift unexpectedness of this substi-
tution is theatrically effective, no doubt; but we
may doubt if it is dramatically sound.   Ibsen has
rooted *Nora's* fascination, felt by every spectator,
in her essential femininity, only at the end to
send her forth from her home, because she
seemed to be deficient in the most permanent and
most overpowering of woman's characteristics —
the maternal instinct.   It may be that she did
right in leaving her children; it may even be that
she would have left them; but up to the moment
when she declared her intention to go, nothing in
the play has prepared the spectator for this
strange move.   Ibsen has failed to make us feel
when the unexpected happened that this, however unforeseen, was exactly what we ought to
have expected.

No fault of this kind can be found with
'Ghosts,' that d:.st' tragedy of a house built
on the quicksa..ls of falsehood, that appalling
modern play with the overwhelming austerity of
an ancient tragic drama, that extraordinarily

compact and moving piece, in which the Norwegian playwright accomplished his avowed purpose of evoking "the sensation of having lived thru a passage of actual life." A few years only before Ibsen brought forth his 'Ghosts,' Lowell had asserted that "That Fate which the Greeks made to operate from without, we recognize at work within, in some vice of character or hereditary disposition"; and Greek this play of Ibsen's is in its massive simplicity, in the economy of its bare structure with five characters only, with no change of scene, with no lapse of time, and with an action that rolls forward irresistibly with inevitable inexorability. As there was something Æschylean in 'Brand' so there is something Sophoclean in 'Ghosts'; altho Ibsen lacks the serenity of the great Greek and Sophocles had a loftier aim than that of evoking "the sensation of having lived thru a passage of actual life." There is no echo in 'Œdipus' of the cry of revolt which rings thru 'Ghosts,' and yet there was a strange similarity in the impression made on at least one spectator of the actual performances of these tragedies, the ancient and the modern, the one after the other, at a few days' interval here in New York,—an impression of deepening horror that graspt the throat and gript the heart with fingers of ice.

The most obvious resemblance between the

Greek tragedy and the Scandinavian social drama is in their technic, in that the two austere playwrights have set before us the consequences of an action, rather than the action itself. Here Ibsen has thrown aside the formula of the " well-made play," using the skill acquired by the study of Scribe in achieving a finer form than the French playwright was capable of, a form seemingly simple but very solidly put together. The structure of 'Ghosts' recalls Voltaire's criticism of one of Molière's plays that it seemed to be in action, altho it was almost altogether in narrative. Ibsen has here shown a skill like Molière's in making narrative vitally dramatic. Ibsen has none of Molière's breadth of humor, none of his large laughter, none of his robust fun; indeed, Ibsen's humor is rarely genial; grim and almost grotesque, it is scarcely ever playful; and there is sadly little laughter released by his satiric portrayals of character. But the Scandinavian playwright has not a little of the great Frenchman's feeling for reality, and even more of his detestation of affectation and his hatred of sham. The creator of *Tartuffe* would have appreciated *Pastor Manders*, an incomparable prig, with self-esteem seven times heated, engrossed with appearances only and ingrained with parochial hypocrisy.

But we may be assured that Molière, governed by the social instinct as he was, would never have shared Ibsen's sympathy for the combatant hero of his next play, that 'Enemy of the People,' with the chief figure of which the dramatist has seemed willing for once to be identified. We may even incline to the belief that Molière would have dismist *Dr. Stockman* as lacking in common-sense, and in the sense of humor, and also as a creature both conceited and self-righteous, pitiably impractical and painfully intolerant. And we are quite at a loss even to guess what the French playwright-psychologist, who has left us the unforgetable figure of *Célimène* would have thought of *Hedda Gabler,* that strangest creation of the end of the century, anatomically virtuous, but empty of heart and avid of sensation.

In 'Hedda Gabler' as in the 'Enemy of the People' Ibsen gives up the Sophoclean form which was exactly appropriate for the theme of 'Ghosts.' With admirable artistic instinct the playwright returns to the framework of the "well-made play" or at least to that modification of the Scribe formula which Augier and Dumas *fils* had devised for their own use. The action has not happened before the curtain rises on the first act; it takes place in the play itself, in front of the spectators, just as it does in the 'Demi-monde.' The exposition is contained in the first act, clearly and completely; the characters are all set in motion before us, *Hedda* and her husband, *Mrs. Elvsted* and *Eilert,* and the sinister figure of *Inspector Brack* in the background. This first act, even to its note of interrogation hung in the air at the end, might have been constructed by Augier,—just as the scene in the second act between *Hedda* and *Brack* recalls the manner of the younger Dumas, even in its lightness and its wit. Yet we may doubt whether any of the modern French playwrights could have lent the same curt significance to this commonplace interview between a married *demi-vierge* and an *homme-à-femmes* ;—of their own accord these French terms come to the end of the pen to describe these French types.

Interesting as 'Hedda Gabler' is on the stage and in the study, suggestive as it is, it cannot be called one of Ibsen's best-built plays. Technically considered it falls below his higher level; it does not sustain itself even at the elevation of the 'Demi-monde' or of the 'Effrontés.' It does not compel us to accept its characters and its situations without question. It leaves us inquiring, and, if not actually protesting, at least unconvinced. We might accept the heroine herself as an incarnate spirit of cruel curiosity, inflicting purposeless pain, and to be explained, even if not to be justified, only by her impending maternity,—which she recoils from and is unworthy

of. But I, for one, cannot help finding *Hedda*
inconsistent artistically, as tho she was a com-
posite photograph of irreconcilable figures. For
example, she shrinks from scandal, yet she burns
Eilert's manuscript, she gives him one of her
pistols, and finally she commits suicide herself,
than which nothing could more certainly provoke
talk. The pistols themselves seem lugged in
solely because the playwright needed to have
them handy for two suicides,—just as *Brack*
walks into *Hedda's* house in the early morning,
not of his own volition, but because the playwright insisted on it. So at the end *Mrs. Elvsted*
could not have had with her all the notes of
Eilert's bulky book, tho she might have had a
rough draft; and she would never have sat down
calmly to look over these notes instead of rushing
madly to the hospital to *Eilert's* bedside. Again,
Inspector Brack, when he hears of *Eilert's* death,
has really little or no warrant in jumping to the
conclusion that *Hedda* is an accessory before the
fact; and even if she was, this would not give
him the hold on her which she admits too easily.
More than once, we find a summary swiftness
in the motives alleged, for things done before
the spectators have time to grasp the reasons
for these deeds, which therefore appear to be
arbitrary. There is a hectic flush of romanticism
in this play, not discernible in any other of Ibsen's

social dramas, a perfervidness, an artificiality, which may not interfere with the interest of the story but which must detract from its plausibility at least and from its ultimate value.

VII

WHATEVER inconsistencies may be detected now and again by a minute analysis of motive, —and after all these inconsistencies are slight and infrequent, — the characters that Ibsen has brought upon the stage have one unfailing characteristic: they are intensely interesting. They are not mere puppets moved here and there by the visible hand of the playwright; they are human beings, alive in every nerve, and obeying their own volition. The breath of life has been breathed into them; they may be foolish or morbid, headstrong or perverse, illogical or fanatic, none the less are they real, vital, actual. And this is the reason why actors are ever eager for the chance to act them. Where Scribe and Sardou and the manufacturers of the "well-made play" give the performers only effective parts, to be presented as skilfully as might be, Ibsen has proffered to them genuine characters to get inside of as best they could,— characters not easy to personate, indeed, often obscure and dangerous. Because of this danger and this doubt, they are all the more tempting to the true artist, who is ever on the alert for a tussle with technical difficulty. The men and women who people Ibsen's plays are never what the slang of the stage terms " straight parts "; they are never the traditional "leading man" and "leading woman"; in a sense they are all of them, male and female, young and old, "character parts," complex, illusive, alluring. They are not readily mastered, for they keep on revealing fresh possibilities the more searchingly they are studied; and this is why the reward is rich, when the actor has been able at last to get inside of them.

Even when he has done this, when he has put himself into "the skin of the personage" (to borrow the illuminating French phrase), the actor cannot be certain that his personation is finally right. No one of Ibsen's characters is presented in profile only, imposing its sole interpretation on the baffled performer. Every one of them is rounded and various, like a man in real life, to be seen from contradictory angles and to be approached from all sides. No one is a silhouette; and every one is a chameleon, changing color even while we are looking at it. Every part is a problem to the actors who undertake it, a problem with many a solution, no one of which can be proved, however assured the performer may be that he has

hit on the right one. To the actor the privilege
of an artistic adventure like this comes but rarely;
and it is prized accordingly. Not often does he
find under his hand material at once fresh and
solid. He feels the fascination of this chance
and he lays hold of it firmly, even tho he has a
haunting fear of failure, absent from the easy,
daily exercise of his professional skill. He rel-
ishes the opportunity to speak Ibsen's wonderful
prose, that dialog which seems to the mere
reader direct and nervous, and which impresses
the actual auditor in the theater as incomparable
in its veracity, its vivacity, its flexibility, its
subtlety, and its certainty; but which only the
actor who delivers it on the stage can praise
adequately, since he alone is aware of its full
force, of its surcharged meaning, and of its car-
rying power.

To act Ibsen is worth while, so the actors
themselves think; and it is significant that it is
to the actors, rather than to the regular managers,
that we owe the most of our chances for seeing
his plays presented on the stage. That Ibsen
offers opportunities not provided in the pieces of
any other modern dramatist is the belief of many
an actor and of many an actress longing for a
chance to rival the great performers who have
gone before, leaving only their fame behind
them. So it is that the 'Pillars of Society' is set

up in our theaters now and again, and that 'Ghosts' may revisit our stage from time to time. So it is that the ambitious leading lady, abandoning the *Camille* and the *Pauline* of a generation or two ago, yearns now to show what she can do as *Nora* and as *Hedda Gabler*, unable to resist the temptation to try her luck also in impersonating these women of the North, essentially feminine even when they are fatally enigmatic.

VIII

THE actors and actresses do get their chance now and again to appear in an Ibsen part, in spite of the reluctance of the regular managers to risk the production of Ibsen's plays in their theaters. This reluctance is not caused solely by an inability to appreciate his real merits; it is magnified by a healthy distrust for the cranks and the freaks who are most vociferous and least intelligent in praise of him,—for Ibsen, like Browning and like Maeterlinck, has suffered severely from the fulsome adulation of the short-haired women and the long-haired men, who are ever exuberantly uncritical. Perhaps the unwillingness of managers to venture their money in staging these Scandinavian social dramas is due also to a well-founded belief that "there is no money in them," —that they are not likely to attract American playgoers in remunerative multitudes, —that they cannot be forced to the long runs to which the theater is now unfortunately committed.

Ibsen is like all other great dramatists in that he has intended his plays to be performed in the theater, by actors, before an audience; and, therefore has he adjusted them most adroitly to the picture-frame stage of the modern playhouse and filled them with characters amply rewarding the utmost endeavor of ambitious players. But the influence of the actor and of the circumstances of the theater is only upon the outward form of the play, while the influence of the spectator is upon its content solely. This influence has been potent upon every true dramatist, who has had ever in mind the special audience for whom his plays were intended, and at whom they were aimed. Sophocles composed his stately tragedies for the cultivated citizens of Athens, seated on the curving hillside under the shadow of the Acropolis; Shakspere prepared his histories and his comedies to hold the interest of the turbulent throng which stood about the jutting platform in the yard of the half-roofed Tudor theater; and Molière, even when he was writing to order for Louis XIV, never forgot the likings of the fun-loving burghers of Paris. No one of the three ever lookt beyond his own time or wasted a thought upon any other than the contemporary audience in his own city. Even tho their plays have proved to possess universality and permanence, they were in the beginning frankly local in their appeal.

But who are the spectators that Ibsen saw in his mind's eye when he imagined his plays bodied forth in the actual theater? He was not a citizen of a great state, as Molière was, and Shakspere; he did not dwell in a great city, exercising his art in close contact with the abounding life of a metropolis. He was a native of a small country, not even independent, and without large towns; he was born in a petty village and there he grew to manhood; in his maturity he wandered abroad and for years abode in exile, an alien, if not a recluse.

Are not the memories of youth abiding? and can any one of us free himself wholly from the bonds of early environment? The audience that Ibsen has ever had in view when he was making his most searching tragedies of modern life, the audience he has always wisht to move and to rouse, morally and intellectually, was such a group of spectators as might gather in the tiny and isolated village where he had spent his boyhood. Ibsen himself may not have been conscious that this was the audience he was seeking to stimulate; indeed, he may never have suspected it; and he might even deny it in good faith. But the fact remains, nevertheless, obvious and indisputable; and it helps to explain not a little that might otherwise remain obscure. It enables us to suggest a reason for a certain closeness of atmosphere sometimes felt in this play or that, and for a certain lack of largeness of outlook, in spite of the depth of insight. It makes us more tolerant toward a certain narrowness, which is often provincial and sometimes almost parochial.

It is not merely that Ibsen's social dramas are all of them intensely Norwegian, peopled solely with natives and having the fiords ever present in the background. It is not merely that he has shrunk from all international contrasts, and from all cosmopolitanism;—and here, no doubt, he has chosen the better part. It is not that he himself has not shaken off the pettiness of the little village where he received his first impression of his fellow-man. It is that altho he has seen the world outside and altho he is thereby enabled to measure the smallness of what he left behind, he cannot forget the inhabitants of Grimstad, individually and collectively. They supply the constituent elements of the audience which he is ever addressing, consciously or unconsciously. It is their limited horizon he wants to enlarge; and it is their lethargy he is longing to shatter.

IX

PERHAPS there is no injustice in holding that much of Ibsen's arrogant and aggressive individ-ualism and self-assertion, is the result of his own youthful solitude and struggle in the little village where the druggist's ambitious apprentice who wrote poetry and who had opinions of his own, soon managed to get on a war-footing with most of his neighbors,—as the late Professor Boyesen recorded from his own observations at the time, explaining that "a small town, where everybody is interested in what his neighbor has for dinner, is invariably more intolerant of dissent, more tyrannical toward social rebels, than a city of metropolitan rank." And even when Ibsen removed to Christiania he did not get out of this atmosphere of pettiness. As Professor Boyesen remarked, again from personal experience, "One hundred thousand village souls do not make a city." And the same compatriot of the dramatist, in dealing with the 'Enemy of the People' de-clared that "each trait bears the indelible mark of a small society, which stunts and cripples the sons of men, making them crabbed and crooked, when in a richer soil many of them might have shot boldly up in the sunlight."

Norway seems to be a land of villages, with a people not yet enlarged and awakened from stifling bigotry. Its social organization still presses painfully on those who wish to do their own thinking; and half a century ago in Ibsen's impressionable youth, the pressure must have been tragic. There is no call for wonder that he should have reacted violently against these fettering restrictions. There is no need to speculate on the reasons why he has failed to feel the extraordinary delicacy of the problem of the equilibrium between the opposing forces, which have a cramping socialism on the one side and an exuberant anarchy on the other. His choice was swift and he exerted his strength unhesitatingly against the chains which had clanked on his limbs in his early manhood. He knew only too well and by bitter experience the hardness of the crust that encased the Norwegian community and he felt the need of blows still harder to break thru and let in a little light. And this is why he is so emphatic in his individualism; this is why he is so fiercely violent in his assertion of the right of every man to own himself and to obey his own will, contemptuous of the social bond which alone holds civilization together.

It is Boyesen, a fellow Norwegian and an ardent admirer of Ibsen's, who has most clearly stated Ibsen's position: "He seems to be in ill humor with humanity and the plan of creation in general (if, indeed, he recognized such a plan), and he devotes himself, with ruthless satisfaction, to showing what a paltry contemptible lot men are, and how aimless, futile, and irrational their existence is on this earth, with its chaotic strivings and bewildered endeavors." . . . "Furthermore, he utterly undervalues what we call civilization, which he regards primarily as an ignominious compromise—a surrender and curtailment of our natural rights and liberties, in return for a paltry security for life and limb." . . . "He has apparently no appreciation of the tremendous struggle, the immense suffering, the deluge of blood and tears, it has cost to redeem the world from that predatory liberty which he admires, and to build up gradually the safeguards of organized society which he so detests."

In other words, Ibsen is not what is called "an advanced thinker"; he is really the most extreme of reactionaries, because he wants to go back to the beginnings of civilization. He is willing to give up the chronometer and to return to the sun-dial.

It would be unfair, of course, to sustain what is here alleged by quoting speeches from his plays, since Ibsen is too completely a dramatist to use any one character merely as a mask thru the mouth of which he might voice his private opinion. But when we consider the whole group of the social dramas and when we disengage the philosophy underlying them and sustaining them, we may venture to deduce the private opinion of the author. And in his letters to Georg Brandes we find this opinion fearlessly exprest: "I have really never had any strong feeling of solidarity; in fact, I have only in a way accepted it as a traditional tenet of faith,—and if one had the courage to leave it out of consideration altogether, one would perhaps be rid of the worst ballast with which one's personality is burdened." In another letter he wrote: "I may as well say the one thing I love in freedom is the struggle for its attainment. Its possession does not greatly concern me."

As Brandes points out, this attitude of Ibsen's is partly a reminiscence of romanticism; and in Ibsen as in Balzac the romanticist is forever wrestling with the realist. There is in Ibsen's writing an echo of that note of revolt, which rings thruout all the romanticist clamor, a tocsin of anarchy, and which justified the remark of Thiers that the Romanticists of 1830 were the forerunners of the Communists of 1871. And the Communists were only putting into practise what Ibsen was preaching almost simultaneously in his correspondence with Brandes: "The state must be abolished. . . . Undermine the idea of the commonwealth; set up spontaneity and spiritual kinship as the sole determining points in a union; and there will be attained the beginning of a freedom that is of some value." This sounds very like a return to Rousseau, almost a century after the futility of Rousseau's theories had been made manifest to all.

There is no denying, however, that Ibsen's doctrine is most appealing to a dramatist, whose business it is to set on the stage the strivings of the individual. Perhaps the drama would be the one surviving art if anarchy should come,—just as it would be certain to die slowly if socialism should succeed. The self-subordination of socialism would be as deadening as the self-surrender of fatalism to that will-power which must ever be the mainspring of a play to move the multitude. Altho it cannot formulate what it feels, the multitude has no relish for extreme measures; it may be making up its mind to turn toward either anarchy or socialism; but it means to move very slowly and it refuses to be hurried.

Here is a reason why Ibsen's plays are never likely to be broadly popular in the theater. The anarchistic element they contain helps to make them more dramatic, no doubt, more vigorous and more vital; but it is dimly perceived by the plain people who form the crowd of theater-goers, and by them it is dumbly resented. The excessive individualism which gives to Ibsen's best plays their tensity of interest is also the cause of their inacceptability to the multitude shrinking from any surrender of the hard won conquests of civilization. There is significance in the fact that Ibsen's plays have totally failed to establish themselves permanently in France, where the esthetic appreciation of his mastery of his art has been keenest and most competent, but where also the value of the social compact is most clearly understood. Not only in France, but in all other countries governed by the Latin tradition of solidarity, Ibsen's doctrine was certain to be unwelcome—even if it might be wholesome. Outside of Scandinavia it is only in Germany that Ibsen has succeeded in winning acceptance as a popular dramatist, perhaps because it was there that the doctrine of individualism was most needed. In Great Britain, and in the United States, where the individual has his rights, altho with no relaxing of the social bond, the performances of Ibsen's plays have been surprisingly infrequent when we consider their delightful craftsmanship, their indisputable power and their unfailing interest.

X

AFTER all, it is not as a philosopher that Ibsen demands attention, but as a dramatist, as a playwright who is also a poet. If it is his weakness that his theory of life is overstrenuous, one-sided and out of date, it is his strength that he has

276

opinions of his own and that he is willing to
face the problems that insistently confront us to-
day. As Mr. Archer has put it tersely and con-
clusively, Ibsen is "not pessimist or optimist or
primarily a moralist, tho he keeps thinking about
morals. He is simply a dramatist, looking with
piercing eyes at the world of men and women,
and translating into poetry this episode and that
from the inexhaustible pageant."

A moralist he must be, if his work is to have
any far-reaching significance, any final value.
Morality is not something a poet can put into his
work deliberately; but it can be left out only at the
poet's peril, since few works of art are likely to be
worth while if they are ethically empty. Ibsen's
inspiration is too rich for it to be void of moral
purport, even tho the playwright may not have
intended all that we read into his work. There
is a moral in 'Ghosts' as there is in 'Œdipus,'
in the 'Scarlet Letter,' and in 'Anna Karénina,'
—a moral, austere and dispassionate. It contains much that is unpleasant and even painful, but—to quote Arnold's praise of 'Anna
Karénina'—nothing "of a nature to trouble the
senses or to please those who wish their senses
troubled." Ibsen's play, like the tragedy of Sophocles, like the severe stories of Hawthorne and
Tolstoi, is not spoon-meat for babes; it is not
for young men and maidens; but as Goethe

asked nearly a century ago, "What business have our young girls at the theater? They do not belong to it ;—they belong to the convent; and the theater is only for men and women who know something of human affairs." It is for these men and these women that Ibsen, with stern self-control, has written his social dramas, that he may force them to look into matters they are willing enough to ignore and to front the facts of life, ugly as these may be.

More than once in the course of this essay has there been occasion to evoke the names of Sophocles, of Shakspere and of Molière, the supreme masters of the dramatic art. To venture upon any comparison with them is to measure Ibsen by the loftiest standard. In his technic alone can he withstand the comparison, for he is the latest and he has profited by all the experiments and achievements of the strong men who came before him; in mere craftsmanship he is beyond question the foremost of all the moderns. It must be said also that in his intellectual honesty, in his respect for the immitigable laws of character, he rarely falls short. He lacks the clear serenity of Sophocles, the depth and the breadth of the myriad-minded Shakspere, the humorous toleration of Molière. The great Greek, the great Englishman, and the great Frenchman, are, all of them, liberal and sane and wholesome, whatever their subject-matter may be; and here it is that the Scandinavian is felt to be inferior. There are few of his social dramas in which we cannot find more than a hint of abnormal eccentricity or of morbid perversity; and this is the reason why the most of them fail to attain the dignity of true and lofty tragedy.

Perhaps it is with Wagner that Ibsen should be grouped, rather than with Sophocles and Shakspere and Molière. They are the two master-spirits of the stage in the nineteenth century. They are both of them consummate craftsmen, having assimilated every profitable device of their predecessors and having made themselves chiefs, each in his own art. And yet with all their witchery and all their power, we may doubt whether their work will resist the criticism of the twentieth century, because there is at the core of it an exaggeration or disproportion which the future is likely to perceive more and more clearly in the receding perspective of time.

(1905.)

THE ART OF THE STAGE-MANAGER

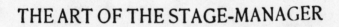

THE ART OF THE STAGE-MANAGER

AS civilization becomes more and more complex, we can find more frequent instances of
"specialization of function," as the scientists
term it.   Only a few years ago, engineering succeeded in getting itself recognized as one of the
professions; and it has already split up into half
a dozen branches, at least, and there are now
not only civil engineers and mechanical engineers and mining engineers, but also electrical
engineers—and even chemical engineers.   The
invention of the steel-frame building has brought
into existence a special class of artizans known as
"housesmiths," a word probably unintelligible
to our British cousins.   Sir Leslie Stephen, in his
delightful 'Studies of a Biographer,' has a
scholarly yet playful paper on the 'Evolution of
the Editor'; and Mr. W. J. Henderson, in his interesting book on the 'Orchestra and Orchestral
Music,' traces the development of the conductor
—the musician whose duties are as important as
they are novel, and who is not now expected to
be able himself to play upon any particular instrument.

"It is impossible to tell when the conductor made his appearance in music," Mr. Henderson asserts. " At the beginning of the seventeenth century, the conductor was at first nothing more than a leader; he was one of the performers whom the rest followed." An inscription in verse on an engraving of a conductor, published in Nuremberg, early in the eighteenth century, declares that "silent myself, I cause the music I control." In the nineteenth century, the conductor had won full recognition as an instrumentalist of a new type, who, without any instrument of his own, played on the whole body of musicians under his command. Of late, he has become so prominent in the eyes of the public, and his personality has been so insisted upon, that there is danger often lest he may distract attention from the music to himself. As Mr. Henderson records calmly: "We have beheld the curious spectacle of people going, to hear not Beethoven or Wagner, but Nikisch or Seidl."

What the conductor is to a performance of orchestral music, the stage-manager is to the performance of a play in the theater. (And in this paper the term "stage-manager" is to be understood as meaning the "producer" of a drama.) His art is as special, as necessary, as novel, and as difficult; and, if it is as yet scarcely recognized and rarely appreciated, this is due in part to the conditions under which his work must be done. The conductor is not only visible but conspicuous; the audience is likely to watch him rather than any one of the musicians he is guiding; whereas the stage-manager must ever be invisible, and is, indeed, most successful if his existence is unsuspected. When the conductor brings a concert to a close, he bows to the applause and then lays down his wand; and all is over. The stage-manager has wrought his wonders, and his labors are practically concluded, before the curtain rises on the first act at the first performance. In this respect, he is like the trainer of a college-crew, who cannot go into the boat with them when the pistol is fired for the race to begin. But everybody is now well aware what it is that the trainer has done for the crew; his portrait appears with theirs in the newspapers and he shares in their glory

Only the expert ever thinks of giving due meed of praise to the hidden stage-manager who is responsible for a more arduous victory in the theater than any ever won on the river. His face is not familiar on the posters; and his name is not in large type on the playbill. All the credit he gets is contained in the single line which records that the play has been "produced" by him. Yet he has been responsible for the entire perform-ance—for the acting and for the costumes, for the scenery and for the properties, for the lighting and for the incidental music; not so much indeed for any one of these things as for the harmony of the whole. If there has been a perfect coördination of all these elements, if there have been no jarring notes, if the spirit of the play has been brought out completely, if everything has gone right from beginning to end, if the whole performance has moved so smoothly as to seem spontaneous, the stage-manager deserves the highest praise for what he has wrought unseen. Yet his sole reward is his own consciousness of work well done, and the chance appreciation of the scanty few who may be competent to estimate the worth of his achievement.

The "producer" of the play, the person who assumes the responsibility for the performance in all its details, may be the dramatist himself; M. Sardou and Mr. Belasco have shown surpassing skill in bringing forth all that lies latent in the inert manuscripts of their plays. He may be the actual manager of the theater; the late Augustin Daly was a stage-manager of striking individuality. He may be the actor of the chief part in the play; Mr. Willard and Mr. Sothern have revealed another aspect of their talent by the artistic manner in which they have staged both new plays and old. He may be at once author and actor and manager, like Mr. Gillette, a past-master of this new and difficult art. Or he may be simply a stage-manager and nothing else, a craftsman of a new calling, not author, not actor, yet able on occasion to give hints to playwright and to player. Here, again, is another resemblance to the conductor, who can impose his own will on the orchestra, altho he may not be able to play one of the instruments in it, and altho he may be quite incapable of composing.

That the task of the stage-manager is more difficult than that of the conductor is due to the fact that the composer has prescribed exactly what share each instrument shall take, the conductor having this full score in his possession; whereas the stage-manager receives from the author only the spoken words of the play, with but summary indications as to the gestures, the movements, the scenery, and so forth. He has not a full score, but only a sequence of themes incompletely orchestrated, and with the missing passages to be supplied at his own discretion. And as the richness of the harmony depends largely upon his ability to amplify properly the hints of the author, the stage-manager is, in fact, almost a collaborator of the playwright; he is forced into a more intimate relation with the dramatist than that which the conductor bears toward the composer. To a collaboration of this sort, ordinary playgoers never give a thought, content to take the performance as they see it, and ready often to credit the actor, not only with the inventions of the stage-manager, but even with those of the author also. They accept the play as it is presented to them, just as tho it had happened, with no suspicion of the forethought by which the performance has been made possible.

George Henry Lewes, in his stimulating essays, 'On Actors and the Art of Acting,' has told us that audiences are inclined to overestimate the genius of an actor and to underestimate his trained skill. We are prone to accept the fallacy of the "inspiration of the moment," and to give little credit to the careful preliminary rehearsing which is at once a humble substitute for inspiration, should this fail to appear, and its solid support, should it happen to present itself. For the thoroness of this preliminary preparation the stage-manager is responsible; and it is at rehearsal that he seeks to bring about the perfect "team-play" which is absolutely necessary,— the subordination of individual display to the larger advantage of the whole performance. The reason why the so-called "all-star revivals" of old plays are often sadly disappointing, is to be found in the absence of this team–play, in the exaggerated self-assertion of the individual actors, whom the stage-manager has been unable to control. Few members of an "all-star" company can be relied upon for the "sacrifice-hits," which the best team-play may now and then demand. And this is why a wise dramatist, if he were put to the choice, would prefer to have his piece performed by a company of average merit directed by a stage-manager of skill and authority, than by far better actors under lax and inefficient stage-management. One of the varied qualifications needed by stage-managers is the insight to estimate the personality of the actors, so that the play may profit by what each of them can do best, while the exuberance of an aggressive individuality is restrained from interfering with the due proportion of the performance.

While it is the duty of the stage-manager to handle all the elements in his control so as to make the performance as perfect as possible, his most important function is to direct the actors themselves, to see that they read their lines intelligently, with just the emphasis requisite at that given moment in the unfolding of the story of the play, and to advise them as to the gestures and movements which should tell this story almost as plainly as the words themselves. Some actors scarcely ever need a hint at rehearsal, reading their speeches naturally the first time and finding for themselves the appropriate by-play,—"business," as technical phrase terms it. Other actors, in no wise inferior in power of per-

sonation, need to be guided and stimulated by
advice; even if not inventive themselves, they
may be swift to take a hint and to wring from it
all its effectiveness. Rachel, probably the greatest
actress of the last century, felt herself lost
without the tuition of Samson, a comic actor
himself, but a teacher of force, originality and
taste. Mrs. Siddons, again, owed some of her
most striking effects to her brother, John Philip
Kemble. It was Kemble who devised for her,
and for himself, the new reading and the business
now traditional in the trial scene of ' Henry VIII,'
where the *Queen* at bay lashes *Wolsey* with the
lines beginning:

Lord Cardinal, to you I speak—

Kemble suggested that the *Queen* should pause,
after the first two words, as tho making up her
mind what she should say. While she hesitates,
the other cardinal, *Campeius*, thinking himself
addrest by a lady, steps forward. The *Queen*,
seeing this, waves him aside with an imperious
gesture, which sweeps forward to *Wolsey*, at
whom she hurls the next words,

To *you* I speak!

and then the rest of the fiery speech pours forth
like scorching lava.

If the older plays, either tragedies or comedies,

seem to us sometimes richer in detail than the more modern pieces, we shall do well to remember that these earlier dramas have profited by the accretions of business and of unexpected readings due to the unceasing endeavor of several generations of actors and of stage-managers. The plays of Shakspere that are most frequently performed, the comedies of Molière also, have accumulated a mass of traditions, of one kind or another, some of these being of hoary antiquity. In ' Hamlet,' for example, in the graveyard scene, it was the habit of the *Second Grave-digger* to take off his coat before beginning his work, and then to proceed to divest himself of an indeterminate number of waistcoats, to the increasing disgust of the *First Grave-digger*. Oddly enough, this same business is traditional in the 'Précieuses Ridicules,' the less important of the two comedians going through exactly the same mirth-provoking disrobing. Probably the business was elaborated for some medieval farce long before Molière was born, or Shakspere either. Of late, it has been omitted from ' Hamlet,' but it is still religiously preserved in the performances of the ' Précieuses ' by the Comédie-Française, the company of actors that Molière founded.

Many another tradition is also cherished at the Français, the origin of which is lost in the mists of antiquity. In the ' Malade Imaginaire,' for ex-

ample, *Thomas Diafoirius* is always provided
with an absurdly high child's chair, apparently
the property of *Louison ;* and in the ' Avare,' after the miser has blown out a candle twice and
finally pocketed it, the custom is for his servant
to sneak behind him and to light the candle once
again as it sticks out of his coat. Regnier, the
cultivated and brilliant comedian (whose pupil
M. Coquelin was in his 'prentice-days), published
a text of Molière's most powerful play. which he
called ' Le Tartuffe des Comédiens ' because he
had recorded in it all this traditional business. M.
Coquelin has told me that he hopes to be able
some day to edit other of Molière's masterpieces
on this principle. And it is greatly to be wisht that
some stage-manager of scholarly tastes would
provide us with a record of the customary effects
to be obtained in the performance of most of Shakspere's plays, as these have been accumulated in
the theater itself. Perhaps this book might be able
to tell us why it is that tradition warrants the
same rather trivial practical joke in the performance of the ' Merchant of Venice,' and in the
performance of ' Romeo and Juliet,'—the business
of embarrassing a servant by repeated bows of
mock courtesy and protracted farewell.

In preparing for a revival of one of the masterpieces of Shakspere, the accomplished stage-
manager of to-day considers all these traditions

inherited from the past, discarding some of them
and selecting those which appear to him worthy
of preservation, and which will accommodate
themselves to the general scheme of the whole
performance as he has conceived it in his mind's
eye. He makes such arrangements as he deems
necessary, devising wholly new effects to fit the
more modern methods of presentation, which are
less purely rhetorical than they were in the
eighteenth century, and more pictorial. When
Herr Barnay impersonated *Mark Antony* in the
Meiningen revival of 'Julius Cæsar,' the novel
stage-management gave freshness to the Forum
scene and greatly increased its force. As *Mark
Antony* ascended the rostrum, after *Brutus* had
asked the mob to listen to him, the crowd was
too highly wrought up over the speech they had
just heard to pay heed to the next speaker. They
gathered in knots praising *Brutus;* and the mur-
mur of their chatter was all the greeting that
Mark Antony received. Herr Barnay stood for
a moment silent and then he began his appeal
for their attention: "Friends—Romans—countrymen—!" but scarcely a citizen listened to him.

   "Lend me your *ears*," he begged, "I come
to bury Cæsar not to praise him!"

   And then the nearest group or two grudgingly
turned toward the rostrum; and to these the
adroit speaker addrest himself, coaxing, cajoling,

flattering,—making frequent pauses, in every
one of which the audience could see another band
of citizens drawn under the spell of his eloquence. When he had them all attentive, he
played on their feelings and aroused their enthu-
siasm; then, after a swift and piercing glance
around to see if they were ripe for it, he brought
forth *Cæsar's* will; and after that *Brutus* was
forgotten, and *Mark Antony* held the mob in the
hollow of his hand to sway it at his will. It
matters little whether the credit of this most ingenious rearrangement was due to Herr Barnay
himself, or to the unseen stage-manager; the spectator could not but recognize that a great play
had received new illumination by it, and that a
certain richness of texture had been disclosed
which had hitherto lain concealed and unsuspected.

Sometimes, it must be confest, this craving
after pictorial novelty overreaches itself. Perhaps the allowable limit was not overstept when
Sir Henry Irving gave *Ophelia* a fan of peacock-
feathers, in order that *Hamlet* might play with
it and have it in his hand when he has to say,
" Ay, a very peacock! "

But it may be doubted whether the boundary
of the justifiable was not crost, when the same
stage-manager had the duel-scene of ' Romeo
and Juliet ' take place in an open square, with its

raised fountain not far from the porch of the cathedral, so that *Mercutio* might be able to point right and left when he declared that his wound would serve, altho it was not "as deep as a well or as wide as a church-door." Pretty as this is and clever, it seems a little petty. To suggest that *Mercutio* was in need of visible promptings for his fancy, is to diminish the quick-wittedness of Shakspere's wittiest character.

Yet, either of these instances will serve to show the searching thoroness with which the stage-manager seeks to project the whole performance in all its minor details, having combined in advance the gestures of the several actors, the movements of each in relation to those of the others, the properties they make use of, and the scenery in the midst of which they play their parts. Altho the scenery, the properties and the costumes are designed by different artists, it is the duty of the stage-manager to control them all, to see that they are harmonious with each other, and that they are subdued to the atmosphere of the "production" as a whole. He subordinates now one and now another, that he may attain the more fitting contrast. Mr. Bronson Howard was one of the authors of 'Peter Stuyvesant, Governor of New Amsterdam,' and to his skilful direction the "production" of the play was committed. The first act took place in a Dutch garden ablaze with autumn sunshine; and, therefore, all the costumes seen in that act were grays and greens and drabs of a proper Dutch sobriety. The second act presented the New-Year's reception at night in the *Governor's* house, and then the costumes were rich and varied, so that they might stand out against the somber oak of the spacious hall.

To the first rehearsal of a play, new or old, the stage-manager sometimes comes with all the salient details of the future performance visualized in advance, knowing just where every character ought to place himself at every moment of the action, and having decided where every piece of furniture shall stand, and how the actors will avail themselves of its assistance. One accomplished stage-manager of my acquaintance, an actor himself, works out with a set of chessmen the intricate problem of moving his characters naturally about the stage. Another, a playwright this one, has a toy theater in which to manœuver the personages of the play into exactly the most effective positions. In one of M. Sardou's pieces, the manuscript of which I once had occasion to study, the chairs stand at the beginning of the first act in very different positions from those in which they are required to be at the end of the act; and the manuscript contained full directions indicating just when and exactly how one or another of the characters should seem accidentally to push a chair into the needed position.

Since modern science has revealed the influence of environment on character, and since modern fiction, following the example set by Balzac, has brought out the significance of the background before which an individual lives, moves and has his being, the stage-manager has a more difficult duty than ever before. He has to see to it that the scenery and all the fittings of the set are congruous, and that they are significant, not merely of the place itself, but of the people also. The late John Clayton showed me the model for the scene of the first act of 'Margery's Lovers,' remarking with a smile of satisfaction that, when the curtain should go up, and before a word had been uttered, everybody in the house would know that the story was laid in Southern France. When the late James A. Herne brought out a play in which husband and wife took opposite sides on the slavery question, the curiously stiff and old-fashioned furniture used in the first act seemed to strike the key-note of the drama; the spectators could not but feel that those who lived amid such surroundings were precisely the persons who would behave in that way.

The stage-manager is encouraged to try for

these pictorial effects, because the stage is now withdrawn behind a picture-frame in which the curtain rises and falls. It is no longer thrust out into the midst of the spectators, as it was in Shakspere's time; nor does it now project beyond the line of the curtain, curving out alongside the stage-boxes, as it did until the third quarter of the nineteenth century. It is now separated from the audience by the straight row of footlights, within the lower border of the frame; and the electric light which reaches every corner of the stage, has put it into the power of the stage-manager to modify his illumination at will, and to be confident that no gesture will be lost no matter how he may arrange his groups against his background. He can darken the whole stage, slowly or suddenly, as he sees fit. Much of the intense effect attained by Sir Henry Irving in the trial-scene of the 'Bells' was due to the very adroit handling of the single ray of light that illumined the haunted burgomaster, while the persons who peopled his fatal dream were left in the shadow, indistinct and doubtful. Perhaps the most moving moment in Mrs. Fiske's production of Paul Heyse's 'Mary of Magdala' was after night had fallen, and when the betrayer knocked at the door of *Caiaphas*, who came forth with a lantern and cast its rays full on the contorted face of the villain,—that face being the sole object visible on the darkened stage, as the *High Priest* hissed forth the single word, "Judas!"

The expert playwright of every period when the drama has flourished abundantly, has always adjusted the structure of his play to conform to the conditions of the theater of his own time; and the more adroit of the dramatists of to-day have been swift to perceive the necessity for a change of method, since the thrust-out platform has been succeeded by the stage behind the picture-frame. They are relinquishing the rhetorical devices which were proper enough on the platform-stage, and which now seem out of place on the picture-stage. They find their profit in accepting as a principle the old saying that "actions speak louder than words." They are abandoning the confidential soliloquy, for example, which was quite in keeping with the position of an actor in close proximity to the spectators,—in the midst of them, in fact,—and which strikes us as artificial and unnatural now that the actor is behind the mystic line of the curtain. They are giving up the explanatory "aside,"—lines spoken directly to the audience, and supposed to be unheard by the other characters on the stage.

In Mr. Henry Arthur Jones's artfully articulated play, 'Mrs. Dane's Defence,' a most ingenious specimen of story-telling on the stage, the harassed heroine, left alone at a crucial moment, did not express her emotion in a soliloquy, as she would have done even fifty years ago. She revealed her agitation solely by the sudden change of her expression and by her feverish movements, which not only betrayed her anxiety, but were really more eloquent than any mere words were likely to be. Even more remarkable examples of the skill with which significant action may be substituted for speech, can be found in 'Secret Service'; and Mr. Gillette has explained that, in the performance of his own plays, he is "in the habit of resorting largely to the effects of natural pauses, intervals of silence,—moments when few words are spoken and much mental struggle is supposed to take place," finding these methods "especially effective at critical junctures." Perhaps no other modern dramatist relies so frankly upon sheer pantomime as Mr. Gillette does; and, certainly, no other has ever made a more skilful use of it. But the tendency can be observed in all our later playwrights, and it will surely increase as the possibilities of the picture-stage come to be better understood.

What the stage-manager is forever striving to attain, in addition to these salient effects, is variety of impression. He seeks to achieve a harmony of tone and to create an intangible atmosphere, in which the spirit of the play shall be revealed. To secure this, he often calls in the aid of music. When Sir Henry Irving produced ' Much Ado about Nothing,' the note of joyous comedy that echoed and reëchoed thruout the performance, was sustained by sparkling rhythms, old English dance-tunes, most of them, that frolicked gaily thru the evening. In Mr. Belasco's production of the Darling of the Gods,' the accompanying music was almost incessant, but so subdued, so artfully modulated, so delicately adjusted to the action, that perhaps a majority of the audience was wholly unconscious of the three Japanese themes which had been insisted upon again and again. To evoke the atmosphere of Japan as soon as possible, Mr. Belasco also had a special curtain designed for the play, which coöperated with the exotic music to bring about a feeling of vague remoteness and of brooding mystery.

But all these effects, audible or visible, may be resented as mere stage-tricks, unless they really belong where they are put, unless they are intimately related to the main theme of the play, and unless they are really helpful in evoking and sustaining the current of sympathy. They are excrescences if they exist for their own sake only; they are still worse if they interfere with this current of sympathy, if they distract attention to themselves. The stage-manager must ever be on his guard against the danger of sacrificing the major to the minor, and of letting some little effect of slight value in itself interfere with the true interest of the play as a whole. At the first performance of Mr. Bronson Howard's 'Shenandoah,' the opening act of which ends with the firing of the shot on Sumter, there was a wide window at the back of the set, so that the spectators could see the curving flight of the bomb and its final explosion above the doomed fort. This scenic marvel had cost time and money to devise; but it was never visible after the first performance, because it drew attention to itself, as a mechanical effect, and so took off the minds of the audience from the Northern lover and the Southern girl, the Southern lover and the Northern girl, whose loves were suddenly sundered by the bursting of that fatal shell.

At the second performance, the spectators did not see the shot, they only heard the dread report; and they were free to let their sympathy go forth to the young couples. Here, once more, as so often in the art of the stage, suggestion was far more potent than any attempt to exhibit the visible object. The truth of this axiom was shown in the third act of the same play, during its earlier performances, when the playwright with the aid of a scant dozen soldiers was able to suggest all tne turmoil and all the hazards of a battle only a little removed. At later performances, the author allowed the attempt to be made actually to represent certain phases of a retreat, with horse, foot and artillery on the stage all at once; and altho the stage-management was excellent in every way, perhaps the total effect was less than when the far larger possibilities of a great battle had been merely suggested to the spectators, their own imaginations evoking the possibilities of war more completely than any stage-manager could set it before them.

So in the ' Tosca' of M. Sardou, the torture of the hero, if we were to see it, might be received with incredulity, but we are far more likely to accept it as real when we perceive it only thru the sufferings of the heroine at the sight of it. So again, in the ' Darling of the Gods,' the destruction of the little band of loyal Samurai is far more effectively conveyed to us by the faint voices which call and answer once and again in the Red Bamboo Forest, than it would be by any actual presentation of combat and carnage. So, in ' L'Aiglon,' the specters on the battle-field of Wagram are much more impressive, if they are merely imagined by the poor little prince, and if there is no vain attempt to realize them concretely. So, in ' Macbeth,' there is a loss of interest if the ghost of *Banquo* struts in upon the banquet.

Our modern incredulity doubts the existence of returning spirits, altho it is willing enough to accept the reality of *Macbeth's* belief in them; but when the play was originally produced, the superstitious groundlings would have felt themselves cheated of an alluring spectacle if the sheeted ghost had not stalked out on the stage to shake his gory locks.

In the spacious days of Elizabeth, the half-roofed theaters were only a little less medieval than the pageants of the mysteries had been; and the task of the stage-manager must have been very simple indeed. There was no scenery, and the performance took place by daylight, so that all the producer of a new play had to do was to arrange such elementary business as was possible on a platform encumbered with an indefinite number of spectators. Like all stage-managers, then and now, he had of course to direct the actors themselves; and *Hamlet's* speech to the *Players* gives us good reason to believe that Shakspere must have been an excellent trainer, however modest may have been his own native gifts as an actor. Molière, like Shakspere in so many ways, was like him in being author and actor and manager; and in the 'Impromptu de Versailles' he has left us a most instructive record of his own methods of rehearsing his own company.

304

But, altho the playhouse in which Molière performed was roofed and lighted, and altho he had some scenery, yet there were spectators sitting on his stage as on Shakspere's, and the conditions were those of the platform and not of the picture. Oddly enough, the most pictorial of all the theaters that have preceded our own time is the theater of the Athenians. Few spectacles can ever have excelled in beauty an outdoor performance in the theater of Dionysius, when the richly-appareled chorus circled into the orchestra, to the sound of music, in the spring sunshine, with the breeze from the Bay of Salamis blowing back their floating draperies, that could not but fall into lines of unexpected delight and ineffable grace. Stage-management, which was necessarily neglected by the great Elizabethans, owing to the rudeness of their playhouses, was studied as an art by the great Greeks and held by them in high esteem. The dramatic poet was himself the producer, training the three actors, arranging the evolutions of the chorus, and accepting full responsibility for the perfection of the complete work of art. Silent himself, he caused the music he controlled.

(1903.)